Free and Low Cost Software for the PC

FREE AND LOW COST SOFTWARE FOR THE PC

by
Victor D. López

McFarland & Company, Inc., Publishers
Jefferson, North Carolina, and London

ISBN 0-7864-0847-2 (softcover : 50# alkaline paper)

Library of Congress cataloguing data are available

British Library cataloguing data are available

©2000 Victor D. López. All rights reserved

Cover image ©2000 Photodisc

No part of this book may be reproduced or transmitted in any form or by any means, electronic or mechanical, including photocopying or recording, or by any information storage and retrieval system, without permission in writing from the publisher.

Manufactured in the United States of America

*McFarland & Company, Inc., Publishers
Box 611, Jefferson, North Carolina 28640
www.mcfarlandpub.com*

For my dear friends,
Maria del Carmen and Torry Granja,
for 30 years of love and support

ACKNOWLEDGMENTS

This book would not be possible without the talented men and women who grace us with the fruits of their labor I have been privileged to review herein. Please support them, and the thousands of other programmers like them, by registering their shareware programs if you continue to use them beyond the allowed evaluation period. For those especially generous souls who ask no compensation for their work and allow us to use it freely to our benefit, I give a special thanks, and I encourage you to give them positive feedback if, like me, you like their work.

I would also like to thank Ken Ansley, who has been more a brother than a friend to me for these past 24 years since our days at Brooklyn Technical High School. Though we both still live in New York, we are separated by nearly 200 miles, making a collaboration on this book impractical. It would have been fun to do it again, Ken. Maybe next time?

A special thanks to Professor Charles Molé, Chair of the Department of Business and Information Technology at SUNY Delhi, for his support and encouragement of my research, writing and pursuit of various academic projects throughout his tenure as chair of my department.

Finally, I would like to thank my wife and best friend, Alice Z. López, for her understanding and support while I researched and wrote this book, and for not questioning the decidedly non-academic, loud, and often annoying sounds of music, explosions and mayhem emanating from my study late into the night for endless weeks as I evaluated programs for inclusion in Unit 5. And thanks too to Mom and Dad (Manuela and Felipe López), just because.

Victor D. López
Oneonta, New York

CONTENTS

Acknowledgments	vii
Introduction	1
UNIT I: UTILITY PROGRAMS	9
1. File Compression Utilities	11
2. Screen Capture Utilities	18
3. Virus Detection and Protection	22
4. System Analysis	32
5. Disk Utilities	36
6. File Utilities	43
7. Mouse Utilities	55
UNIT II: PERSONAL PRODUCTIVITY	61
8. Loan Calculators	63
9. Printer Tools	70
10. Time Tools	76
11. Personal Information Management	83
UNIT III: EDUCATIONAL PROGRAMS	89
12. Testing and Training Aids	91
13. Speed Reading	98
14. Courseware	102
15. Grading Programs	106

Also unchanged is the non-refundable nature of software packages. Unlike most other consumer purchases for which retailers typically readily allow exchanges or refunds, buyers buy expensive software packages at their own risk, often sight unseen. If you are trying to decide whether Lotus Millennium Suite, Microsoft Office 2000 or Corel Office 2000 is best for you, you must often depend on third party reviews in trying to decide which package best suits your needs. Given that such leading packages often list for around $500 and retail for about $300 (street prices as of this writing), making a wrong choice can be a frustrating, time consuming and expensive proposition. If you need a copy of these packages you have no choice but to purchase it based on the reputation of the companies that produce them and the recommendation of friends and reviewers.

I have owned and used copies of the Lotus, Corel and Microsoft products for years and am very fond of each, but, though I have my own preferences and opinions of these products, they are often not the same as the "conventional wisdom" reviews offered about them by popular media reviewers who often concentrate on features and speed in their evaluations. The program with the best features and most awards won't necessarily be the best product for you if you don't need or want many of the features or if you find the basic program interface awkward to use. Market share and price are also not necessarily reflective of a program's true value, in my view.

Fortunately, not all software purchases need be made with blind reliance on others' opinions. Many worthwhile programs are available for trial before you buy, and some are available completely free of charge, no strings attached. Many software developers opt to make either full or limited versions of their programs available to the public for evaluation purposes free of charge. Others go even farther, giving away the programs they create. All of the programs in this book fall into one of these two broad categories, and all are available for evaluation free of charge.

Free and User Supported Software Defined

There are essentially three types of software available free of charge: public domain, shareware and commercial demo programs. It is important to understand the distinction between these basic software types, for the type of software involved limits a user's legal rights with regard to its use.

Public domain software, also referred to as freeware, is software that has been released by its creator for use by the general public without the expectation of compensation. Most programmers who release software as freeware retain some rights with respect to it and place restrictions on its further use, such as limiting the ability of others to sell it for a profit or to incorporate its code into programs they write. Keep in mind that software, like all intellectual property, is subject to copyright protection as soon as it is created and saved in some permanent form (such as on a hard or floppy disk) by its creator. This means that such software can only be used to the extent and in accordance with the author's release. As with all software, you must read licensing information provided by the author in order to determine the specific rights you have with respect to its use. Generally speaking, though, freeware requires no payment to the author and may be copied and redistributed freely, though the fee that can be charged for distributing such software is often restricted.

Shareware, also commonly referred to as user supported software, is not released for general use; rather, it is released for evaluation purposes, usually for a specific period of time (e.g., a 30 day evaluation, or a specific number of uses). Authors of shareware expect to get paid for their work, but agree to allow users a free look at their creations for evaluation purposes. If you obtain a copy of a shareware package, you are free to use it and redistribute it in accordance with the author's licensing agreement, but you are legally and morally obligated to register the program after the specified evaluation period, or after a reasonable time when no time period is specified. If you do not wish to register shareware programs, you should uninstall them from your system when the evaluation period expires. If you wish to keep using the program after the evaluation period, then you must send the author whatever fee he or she requires. After submission of the fee, the author may send you an unrestricted copy of the program or may simply forward to you a numeric or alpha-numeric code that you enter at bootup to unlock the program and remove any shareware restrictions it might contain.

Demos (or software demonstration programs) are similar to shareware programs, though these are usually provided by commercial software distributors and, typically, represent a scaled-down, limited version of their full commercial programs. The nomenclature is not important; in fact, some shareware distributors call their programs demos, and some commercial distributors refer to their commercial demo programs as shareware. Generally, however, demos and shareware differ in two specific ways: first, demos are almost always distributed by commercial vendors as a means of increasing interest in their software products by allowing users to sample a limited version of their programs in the hope they will like them and go on to purchase the full version through their local retailer or directly from the vendor; and second, demos almost always provide a severely restricted version of the program, in contrast to shareware which often provides fully functional versions of the programs with few restrictions. To put it another way, shareware is a means of marketing software from vendors directly to consumers, while demo programs are a means of advertising used by commercial vendors to increase interest in the programs they market.

Limits on User Supported Programs

While freeware programs are always fully functional and offered without limitations, the limitations of shareware programs vary widely, often reflecting the faith of their creators in their software and in the willingness of the public to pay for it after a fair trial. Some shareware programs are completely unlimited in functionality when compared with their registered counterparts, while others are severely limited in function or in the duration of the trial license. Most shareware programs, not surprisingly, fall somewhere in between. In evaluating programs for inclusion in this book, I have steered away from programs that I considered unreasonably restricted, and programs burdened with overly intrusive schemes to encourage their registration, such as cumbersome reminders to register that pop up at various times during the running of a program and interfere with its reasonable use, overly long delays in running programs with reminders to register, unreasonably brief evaluation periods, and programs so limited as to be nearly useless in their shareware or demo forms. Some otherwise excellent programs were omitted for this reason alone. Also omitted were commercial demos that do not provide a user the ability to test the program, but merely provide a multimedia commercial of the product. Spending an hour to download a large demo only to find it contains a glitzy commercial for a software product, rather than a trial version of the program itself, is a waste of time and bandwidth.

Program Selection Criteria

The programs that follow have been selected from an incredibly extensive and diverse field of software offerings to be representative of the types of programs currently available. They are but the tiny tip of an enormous iceberg and are among my personal favorites. Although I have examined literally thousands of shareware programs over the past 15 years, it was not my intent in writing this book to identify the very best, but rather to provide the reader with a broad cross section. Indeed, many award winning programs that make the "best of shareware" lists of computer magazines have not been included for a wide variety of reasons ranging from the limited or technical scope of programs, overly restrictive shareware licenses, registration fees that I considered unreasonable, or, in some cases, simply a personal judgment different from that of other reviewers. Thus, while many of the programs included in the pages that follow are, in fact, winners of multiple awards and highly touted by some of the leading computer magazines, others are relatively unknown and some are downright obscure. For each program included here, dozens if not hundreds of others could have been included as well. Any one of the 22 chapters in this book could easily have been expanded into a complete book. My intent is not to present you with a complete feast of the exceptional programs available, buy rather to serve up a tiny morsel as an appetizer that I hope will whet your appetite and encourage you to seek out and discover your own favorites from the ever-expanding choices available.

Sources of Freeware, Shareware and Demo Programs

There are essentially three sources from which you can obtain copies of the tens of thousands of free and user supported programs available for Windows 95/98 and most other operating systems: authors' web pages, shareware download sites and CD-ROM collections.

The author's web page, where available, is the best and most reliable source to find the latest version of a specific software title; where available, I have listed the current official web page for all software reviewed in this text. By the time you read this, newer versions of some programs may be available, and you will find these first at the program's official web page. Some web pages may also change, so don't be surprised if a few of the listed links are inoperable in the future (all have been tried and work as of this writing). If that happens, turn to your favorite search engine for help in locating the program's new official web page. By seeking out a program's official web page, you will also be able to view other software the same author or company may have available for evaluation. And, although the quality and scope of web pages can vary greatly, many authors provide valuable resources such as support, help files, Frequently Asked Question (FAQ) files, add-on programs and the latest registration fee for programs that require registration. Some sites are a veritable treasure trove of goodies that will take you many hours to fully explore and exploit; when you download the latest copy of the leading Microsoft and Netscape browsers reviewed here, for example, take a look at the wonderful supporting programs, documentation, useful links and other terrific features you will find at http://www.microsoft.com and http://www.netscape.com.

Home pages devoted to your favorite programs are terrific when you know the specific program you want or want to explore the family of products that a specific company or programmer has available. But these aren't much use if you are looking to discover new programs. If you have a relatively fast modem (56K or better) or if you have access to the net via a fast network connection, you can surf the Web for new programs with the help of your favorite search engine. If you execute the search for "free software" or "shareware downloads" you will be led to numerous sites from which you can further explore current offerings in freeware, shareware and commercial demo programs. To get you started, I would like to suggest three of my favorite sites: http://www.download.com, http://www.shareware.com and http://www.winfiles.com. In addition, most computer magazines maintain home pages that will either provide you with direct access to their favorite free software titles or with links to sites that offer quality collections of free and user supported software. Some of my favorite computer magazine sites include http://www.pcmagazine.com, http://www.byte.com and http://www.cshopper.com. These sites will not only provide you with free downloads of their favorite programs, but also let you access their collections of invaluable computer-related information.

The third and final source of free software programs is provided by readily available, inexpensive collections sold on CD-ROM by a variety of vendors. These are available from a variety of sources ranging from Internet auctions to commercial software vendors. A good CD-ROM collection has the benefit of being immediately accessible without the need to download or search for programs on-line. Shareware, demo and freeware collections are sold nearly everywhere that software is sold, though they are not always clearly labeled as such. If you look carefully at software collections that are very inexpensive (typically $10 or less for a CD-ROM), the fine print will often identify the program or programs as shareware, demos, or free software. By all means buy a few of these to try (I have amassed quite a collection of such programs over the years). Because shareware and public domain programs are freely distributable, many companies (and some enterprising individuals) have been producing "free software" collections for many years. But remember that the best, cheapest, largest and most current source of such programs is always the Internet.

A Word to Librarians

If you would like to make free software collections available to the general public and have an Internet connection, it is perfectly legal for you to permit copies of any freeware, shareware or demo program to be downloaded for personal evaluation. You may even create a collection of free and user supported software of your own choosing and circulate it on floppy disk or CD-ROM, or sell it at a modest profit to help raise funds to support your library. The only proviso is that you must honor the distribution limitations placed on the software by its author, which typically requires that the software must be distributed with all accompanying files and documentation unchanged and limits the charge that may be made for copying and distributing the software. Should you choose to download and install shareware into the library's computers, however, you must honor the same restrictions as anyone else, which means that you must not use any program beyond its evaluation period, if one is stated, or you will be in violation of the author's copyright. For this reason, I would encourage allowing patrons to download but not install restricted shareware titles. Unrestricted demos and unrestricted freeware programs that are released into the public domain do not pose a copyright problem and may be installed and used within the library indefinitely. As always, if in doubt, read the program's licensing documentation.

CHAPTER 1
FILE COMPRESSION UTILITIES

File compression programs became very popular in the 1980's, when disk storage was both limited and expensive. By using file compression software, the space that files require for storage can typically be reduced by approximately 30% to 90%, depending on the type of file involved and the compression software used. Once files are compressed, they generally cannot be accessed without first decompressing them—a process that requires the use of a file compression utility program.

The sharp drop in the price of mass storage devices such as hard disks, writeable and rewritable CD-ROMS, floptical disks, tape drives and similar devices have made file compression less attractive as a means of saving disk space. Yet, as anyone who regularly surfs the Web knows, most files downloaded from FTP sites or bulletin boards today are compressed—not so much to save disk space but to save time in transmitting files over slow modems and overcrowded networks. Some of these files are self-extracting; to expand them, you need only double-click on the file in Windows Explorer, which then automatically decompresses and installs all archived programs onto your hard disk. Compressed files that are not self-extracting require you to decompress them by using a stand-alone file compression/decompression program. This does not present a problem for experiences users who have been using such programs for years. Less experienced users, on the other hand, can have a difficult time with archived programs, particularly when dealing with older programs that may not be archived by the more common compression utilities such as PKZIP and PKUNZIP. Fortunately, there are a number of freeware and

12 Unit I : Utility Programs

shareware utility programs currently available that simplify the process for expert and novice users alike.

WinZip® Version 6.3

WinZip for Windows 95/98 version 6.3 is one of the most flexible, useful, and full-featured file compression programs on the market.

WinZip presents an elegant solution for power users and casual Web browsers alike. It provides enough flexibility to satisfy anyone's file compression needs with a user-friendly interface that demystifies the process. The program allows for seamless expansion of many popular file formats, including ARC, ARJ, LZH, BinHex, MIME, Xxencode, GZIP, Unix Compress, UUEncode, and the popular ZIP format. It can also create self-extracting archives so that compressed files can be shared with anyone, whether or not they have access to file decompression programs. For Internet browsing, WinZip can be configured to work with both Netscape's Navigator/Communicator and Microsoft's Internet Explorer for automatic

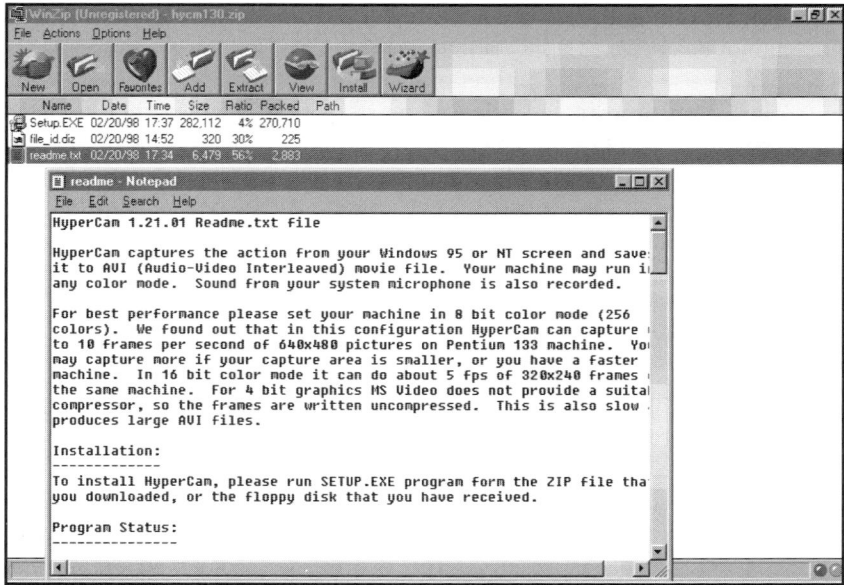

Figure 1.1: WinZip allows you to view the contents of any archived file without first decompressing it. Here, the Readme.txt file of HyperCam, a screen capture utility program downloaded from the Internet in ZIP archived format can be viewed simply by double-clicking on it.

decompression of downloaded files. It can also be configured to work with your favorite virus scanner program to automatically scan for viruses in archived files as they are decompressed, an important feature if your virus scanning program does not automatically warn you of potential viral infections as they occur.

Once installed, WinZip is accessible from your Start Button and can even be launched automatically by double-clicking on any archived file while using Windows Explorer. Its pull-down menus, power buttons and supported drag-and-drop operations make this powerful program easy to use. It even allows you to view the contents of archived files before you decompress them, allowing you, for example, to read text files within compressed files by double-clicking on them without having to take the time or disk space to decompress them first. (See Figure 1.1)

If you're looking for a single program to solve all of your data compression, decompression and file archival needs, you need look no further than WinZip.

Program Name:	WinZip® Version 6.3 © 1991–1997
Program Type:	Shareware (Must register if continue to use the program after a reasonable period of evaluation.)
Company Name:	Niko Mak Computing, Inc.
Company Address:	P.O. Box 540, Mansfield CT 06268-0540
Registration Fee:	License fees vary from $28 for a single computer to as little as $4 each for 500 computers or more.

General Evaluation: WinZip Version 6.3

	Excellent	*Good*	*Average*	*Poor*
Utility	***			
Ease of Use	***			
Ease of Learning	***			
Documentation			***	
Overall Rating	***			

PowerZip® Version 4.01

PowerZip is another solid implementation of an archival utility. It is both powerful and easy to use and contains a very useful on-line help system that makes learning to use the program nearly effortless.

After it is installed, PowerZip can be used directly by running the

Unit I : Utility Programs

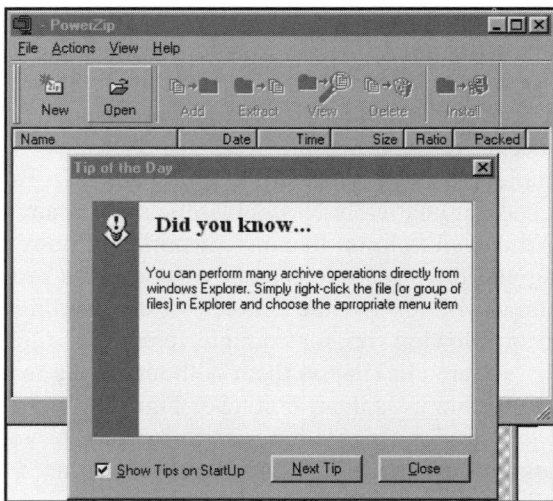

Figure 1.2: PowerZip provides a useful tip every time it is run. This feature can be turned off when the 13 available tips have been viewed.

program from the Windows Start Menu. Once loaded, the program gives a user a full range of options, including the ability to view and run archived files, add or delete files from a compressed archive, and create new compressed file archives. The program supports the ZIP file format directly for archival compression and decompression, as well as TAR, GZIP, and Unix Compress.

PowerZip can also be accessed from Windows Explorer, automatically decompressing archived files if you double-click on them and creating compressed archives of selected files if a user right-clicks with the mouse and then selects "Add to Zip" as an option. If a single file is thus selected, a compressed file will be created with the same name as the selected file and the ZIP file extension; if more than one file is selected, the program will prompt the user for a name for the archive into which the compressed files will be saved. It also provides support for creating self-extracting files for use under DOS and Windows 95/98.

The unregistered version of PowerZip can be used without cost for an unlimited period of time by home users, as well as by users in government, non-profit and educational organizations. The program, must be registered only by commercial users. Links to PowerZip's web page and on-line registration can be accessed directly through the program's help menu.

If you download only one freeware archival program for personal use, this should be it. Highly recommended.

Chapter 1 : File Compression Utilities

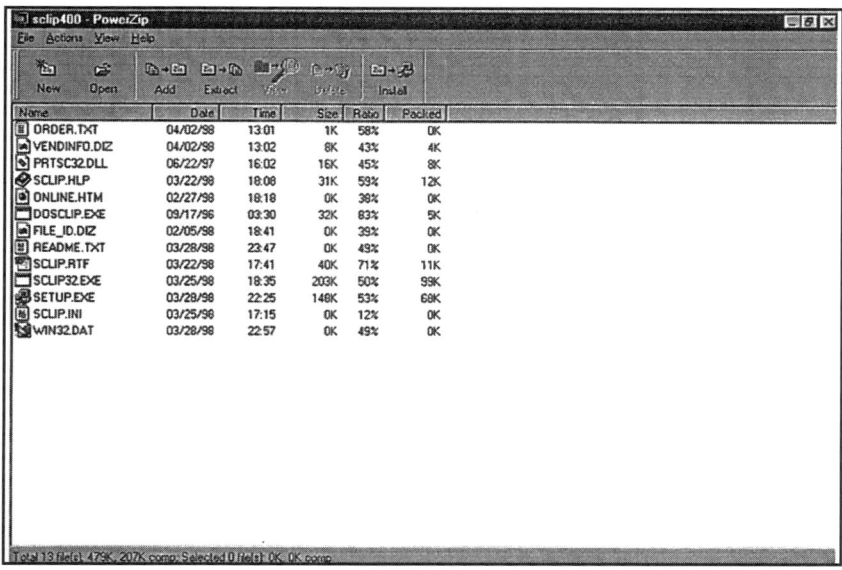

Figure 1.3: PowerZip allows for the easy viewing and updating of any ZIP archive. Files may be viewed and programs run without having to first decompress them. Existing ZIP files can be accessed and new ZIP compressed files created from within Windows Explorer, and drag and drop operations are fully supported.

Program Name: PowerZip® Version 4.01 © 1997-98
Program Type: Freeware (non-commercial use)
Copyright Owner: Dimitri Ternovski
Company Address: N/A
Web Page: http:// www.powerzip.ico.net
Registration Fee: None for non-commercial users (Commercial users: $20 for 1 copy; $80 for 10 copies; $150 for 50 copies. Contact webmaster@powerzip.ico.net for price information on more than 50 copies.)

General Evaluation: PowerZip Version 4.01

	Excellent	Good	Average	Poor
Utility	***			
Ease of Use	***			
Ease of Learning	***			
Documentation	***			
Overall Rating	***			

FASTZip 98® *Version 2.0*

Users who want a free, easy to use file compression utility to compress and decompress ZIP files need look no further than FASTZip 98. While it does not offer all the full range of features and support for multiple file formats found in other archival packages, FASTZip 98 provides an easy to use user interface that includes both pull-down menus and power buttons to make creating compressed archives and decompressing ZIP both fast and uncomplicated, while offering some very useful features that include the ability to create self-extracting archives, view, edit and run files in archives without first decompressing them, and the use of drag and drop file operations. It even provides information on the size of compressed and uncompressed files right from its file menu (see Figure 1.4).

Overall, FASTZip 98 is a terrific program in a small package (it takes up under 1 megabyte of disk space when fully installed) that offers features usually found only on more powerful archival utility programs. When you factor in the freeware nature of the program (no registration is required), FASTZip 98 becomes an irresistible choice for users whose needs it meets.

Program Name: FASTZip 98® Version 2.0 © 1998
Program Type: Freeware (No registration fee or limitation on use.)
Company Name: FastWare
Company Address: N/A
E-Mail: fastware@fastware.se
Web Page: http:// www.fastware.se
Registration Fee: None

General Evaluation: FASTZip 98 Version 2.0

	Excellent	*Good*	*Average*	*Poor*
Utility	***			
Ease of Use	***			
Ease of Learning		***		
Documentation				***
Overall Rating	***			

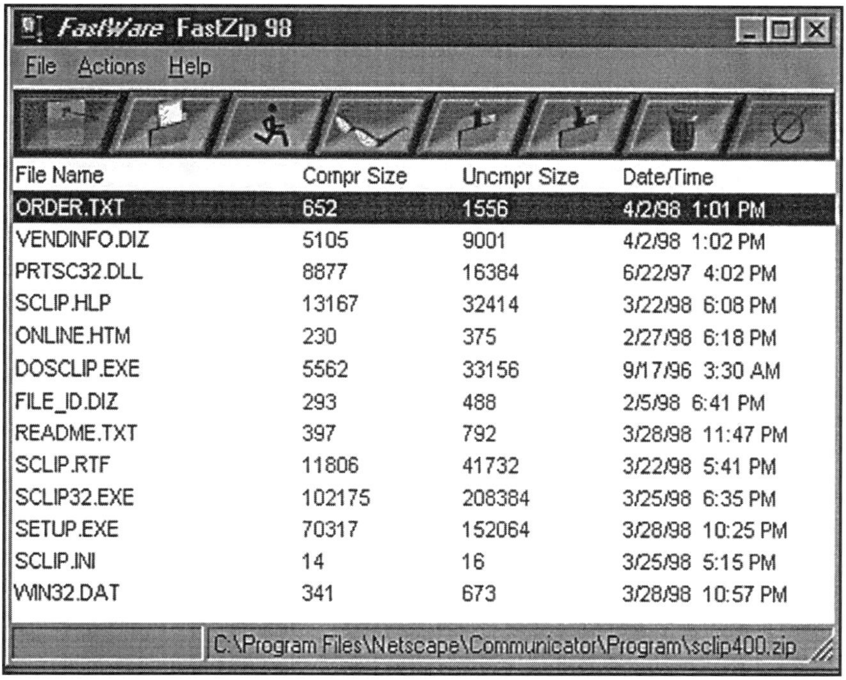

Chapter 1 : File Compression Utilities

File Name	Compr Size	Uncmpr Size	Date/Time
ORDER.TXT	652	1556	4/2/98 1:01 PM
VENDINFO.DIZ	5105	9001	4/2/98 1:02 PM
PRTSC32.DLL	8877	16384	6/22/97 4:02 PM
SCLIP.HLP	13167	32414	3/22/98 6:08 PM
ONLINE.HTM	230	375	2/27/98 6:18 PM
DOSCLIP.EXE	5562	33156	9/17/96 3:30 AM
FILE_ID.DIZ	293	488	2/5/98 6:41 PM
README.TXT	397	792	3/28/98 11:47 PM
SCLIP.RTF	11806	41732	3/22/98 5:41 PM
SCLIP32.EXE	102175	208384	3/25/98 6:35 PM
SETUP.EXE	70317	152064	3/28/98 10:25 PM
SCLIP.INI	14	16	3/25/98 5:15 PM
WIN32.DAT	341	673	3/28/98 10:57 PM

C:\Program Files\Netscape\Communicator\Program\sclip400.zip

Figure 1.4: Once a ZIP compressed file is selected, FASTZip shows the compressed archive's contents, as well as the size of every file in it both in its current compressed state and in its expanded state. For example, the file SETUP.EXE takes up 70,137 bytes of disk space in its current compressed state and will take up 152,064 bytes of disk space once decompressed. Compressed text files can be viewed or edited while in a compressed archive, and compressed program files can be run directly from the FASTZip menu without the need to decompress the entire archived ZIP file. In addition, individual files can be added to or deleted from a ZIP archive at any time, thus permitting users to easily update ZIP archives.

Chapter 2
SCREEN CAPTURE UTILITIES

For those who believe the old adage that "a picture is worth a thousand words," a screen capture utility program will be an invaluable tool. These programs permit a user to capture the contents of part or all of whatever is on the computer screen and save it as a graphics file that can then be printed, inserted into presentation software packages, word processing documents or converted into slides for group presentations. While the best known of these products are offered by commercial vendors, in this chapter we'll examine two shareware and freeware offerings that will fit the needs of most any user.

SuperClip® Version 4.0

Windows 95 incorporates simple screen capture capability through the Print Screen key. By pressing the Print Screen key while a program is running, a copy of the entire screen is sent to the Windows Clipboard. From there, it can be viewed or saved as a BMP file using the Clipboard Viewer. Such images can also be edited by Windows Paint or any other image editing software package. The quickest way to insert a snapshot of a screen into any Windows 95/98 program is to use the Print Screen key to copy an image of the screen to the clipboard, then paste it into whatever file you wish it to appear, where it can then be easily resized or edited. This is the primary process used in capturing images for this text; screen images are copied from the programs being evaluated, then pasted into

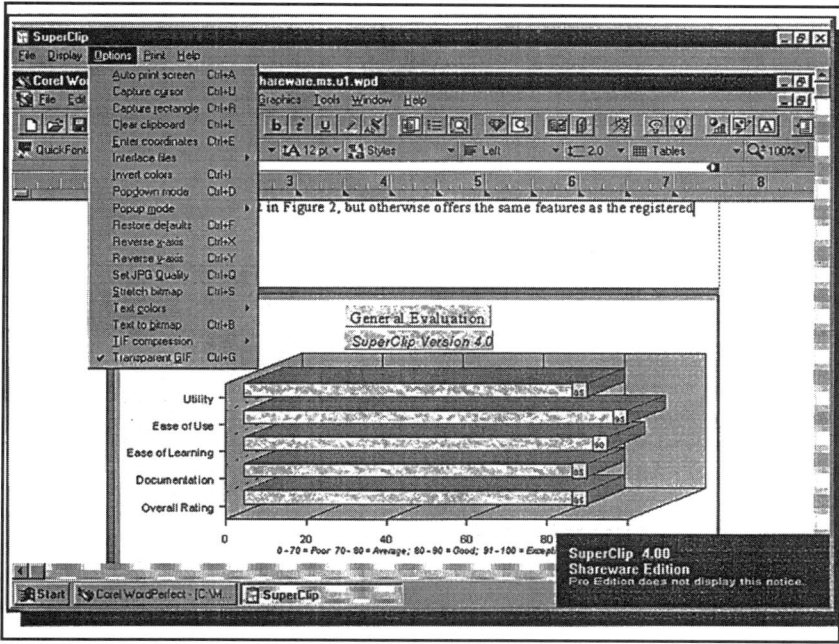

Figure 2.1: *SuperClip 4.0 captured image of a word processing page. Note that the pull-down menu would not normally appear but is shown here for purposes of illustration. Also note the Shareware notice that automatically prints with each captured page but would not print in the registered version.*

the word processing document, sized and edited to achieve the sample screens reproduced throughout the book. It is the most efficient means of working with large numbers of captured screens in a word processing file if you have a word processing package that offers powerful graphics editing capabilities such as WordPerfect or MS Word. But if you are nor comfortable with editing graphics files directly, or prefer greater flexibility in the way that graphics screens are captured and saved, then a dedicated screen capture utility will certainly prove a useful tool. Of the many DOS and Windows-based screen capture utilities I have tried and used over the past decade, SuperClip is one of the best due to its simplicity and ease of use.

SuperClip works as an enhanced clipboard viewer that allows a user to save a captured screen graphics file under six popular graphics file formats (BMP. GIF, JPG, PCX, PNG and TIF). Once loaded, the program works in the background and allows the capture of full screens by pressing the PrtSc key, as well as the capture of the active window by pressing the Alt+PrtSc key combination. SuperClip also permits the capture of screens from DOS programs running in a window. The program also includes DosClip, a memory resident utility program that can be used to capture DOS screens when DOS programs are run in native mode.

Once an image is captured, SuperClip allows you to do some basic editing prior to saving it under one of the six supported file formats. Graphics images can easily be cropped by selecting portions of the captured screen with your mouse or by typing in the precise coordinates through your keyboard, a useful feature when you wish to save only a portion of the captured screen.

In addition to its screen capture capabilities, SuperClip supports the automatic printing of graphics and text screens directly to the printer when the Auto Print Screen Option is selected from the program's Option Menu; when enabled, this feature sends a copy of your screen directly to the printer whenever the PrtSc key is pressed.

SuperClip supports both VGA and SVGA, if a VESA driver is installed. The maximum supported resolution is 1280 x 1024 with 16,777,200 colors. The unregistered shareware version of the program prints the words SuperClip with any captured screen, as you can see on the sample captured text in Figure 2.1, but otherwise offers the same features as the registered version of the program.

Program Name: SuperClip® Version 4.0 © 1994-98
Program Type: Shareware (Must register if continue to use the program after a 15-day evaluation period.)
Company Name: AndroSoft.
Company Address: 125 N. Prospect Street, Washington, NJ 07882
E-Mail: 73140.3340@compuserve.com
Registration Fee: $39 for one computer, $10 for each additional PC or LAN workstation.

General Evaluation: SuperClip Version 4.0

	Excellent	*Good*	*Average*	*Poor*
Utility		***		
Ease of Use	***			
Ease of Learning	***			
Documentation			***	
Overall Rating			***	

Screen Capture® Version 1.4.7

Screen Capture is one of the simplest, easiest to use utilities of its kind and, best of all, it is distributed as freeware, so there is no registration fee.

To use Screen Capture, you double-click on its program icon through Windows Explorer. The program then opens with a pop-up menu screen that allows you to choose from a variety of screen capture options that include capturing the entire screen, the active window, or any portion of the screen selected with the mouse. Once a screen is captured, it can be saved as a BMP file or sent directly to the printer.

Screen Capture is not the most powerful screen capture utility available, and comes with no documentation. But it is very easy to use, works well and costs nothing. What more can one ask?

Program Name: Screen Capture® Version 1.4.7 © 1996-98
Program Type: Freeware (No registration fee or limitation on use. The author accepts voluntary contributions from users wishing to make them.)
Company Name: Nestegg Software
Company Address: N/A
E-Mail: support@nestsoft.com
Web Page: http://www.nestsoft.com
Registration Fee: None

General Evaluation: Screen Capture Version 1.4.7

	Excellent	Good	Average	Poor
Utility		***		
Ease of Use	***			
Ease of Learning	***			
Documentation				***
Overall Rating		***		

CHAPTER 3

VIRUS DETECTION AND PROTECTION

If you're reading this book, chances are that you are already very familiar with computer viruses and might even have had some first-hand exposure to these pesky, often destructive programs at home, work or school. Though the exact number of viruses can never be known, since new ones pop up regularly, it is clear that their number is staggering. The version of MacAfee's Virus Scan reviewed in this chapter, for example, states it has added support for 293 *new* viruses since the software's previous release.

Computer viruses spread by attaching themselves to files and/or disks used in a computer that is infected. Thus, a virus can be spread by unwittingly loading program or data files from infected floppy disks, by reading e-mail that carries with it a hidden virus, or by downloading files from a bulletin board, FTP site or simply by browsing the Internet. Once a virus infects a system, it can lay dormant for some time before actually being noticed, giving a user whose computer is infected the opportunity to unwittingly spread the virus to other uninfected computers through a local network, the Internet or simply through passing infected disks to others.

Not all viruses are destructive. Some have rather harmless purpose, such as embedding a hidden, banal message into your files or software that you pass on to others or displaying a preset message on your computer screen. Others have more ominous purposes, such as reformatting your hard disk, deleting data, altering information in your CMOS file and similar potentially destructive tasks that can obliterate your hard disk's data and programs or give you some very real system configuration headaches.

As long as there are sophomoric or psychopathic hackers, viruses will continue to be a source of concern for all computer users. Short of shutting down your system and dusting off your old electric typewriter and scientific calculator in lieu of your current office suite of applications, there is no way to completely prevent a virus from infecting your system and potentially damaging your data. Fortunately, less drastic measures are available for dealing with the problem, including the excellent virus detection and removal programs that follow, all of which can be evaluated without cost.

Virus Scan® Version 3.12

McAfee's Virus Scan and Virus Shield programs have earned an excellent reputation among devoted users for many years. The early versions of the program were available only for use under DOS and were not always easy to use. With the current 32-bit versions of these programs available for Windows 95/98 and Windows NT, McAfee has combined their state of the art, highly reliable virus detection and protection engine with a very user-friendly environment that is highly customizable to suit any user's personal needs and preferences.

Ease of use and user customization are two hallmarks of this package. In its default configuration, the program automatically scans for viruses and removes them if they are found on the boot disk every time the computer is started. It also installs Virus Shield, the memory-resident portion of the program that works in the background to automatically detect any virus that attempts to attach itself to your system as you work. If a virus is detected, the program will warn you and give you options for dealing with the infected file (e.g., erasing it, or removing the virus and continuing). For users who surf the Web on a regular basis, this is a very useful feature, since the program can warn of potential virus infections from files downloaded from the Internet or even from cookies (small programs that carry graphics, text or other information from a web site to your browser) that can also transmit computer viruses.

Perhaps Virus Scan's most appealing feature is the large number of viruses it recognizes and can remove from infected files—usually without the need to destroy the infected file or program. Registered users can download new virus definition updates from McAfee's World Wide web site (http://www.mcafee.com). An evaluation copy of the program can

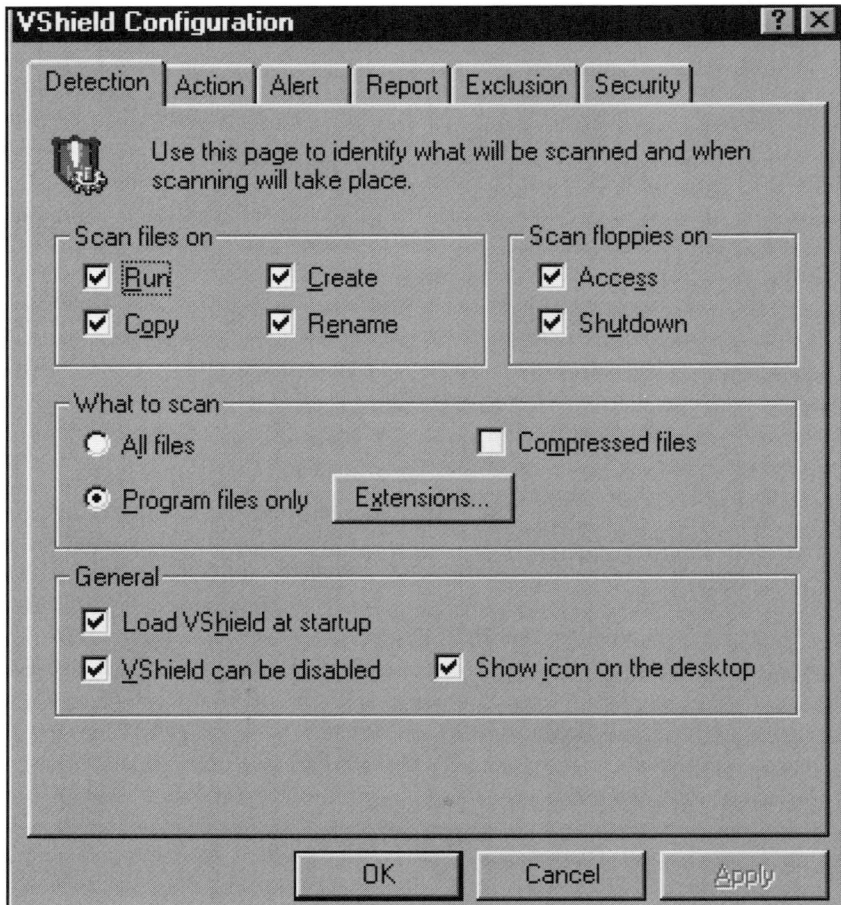

Figure 3.1: Virus Scan offers users a high degree of control over the program's operation. The way the program operates, the types of files, drives and directories it scans and what the program does when a virus is detected can all be changed by the user to meet individual preferences. Less experienced users can simply run the program with its default settings and still obtain a high level of protection.

also be downloaded free of charge from McAfee's home page and used for evaluation purposes for 30 days. After the evaluation period, users must either register the program or stop using it and uninstall it from their computers. (The shareware version of the program can also be downloaded free of charge from many shareware distribution sites on the Net.)

During my 30-day evaluation of the program, I tested it with a variety of viruses, new and old, collected over the past year from infected disks

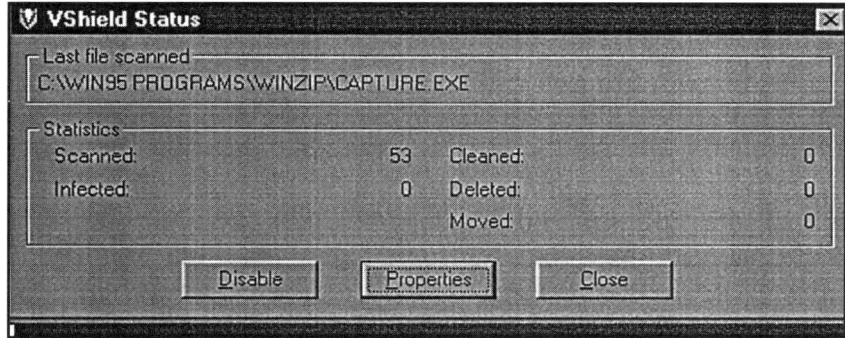

Figure 3.2: Once Virus Scan is installed, the program automatically launches Virus Shield each time the computer is started. Unless disabled, Virus Shield runs in the background, constantly checking for new virus infections as you work. If a virus is detected, the program warns you and can then erase the infected file or remove the virus at your prompting.

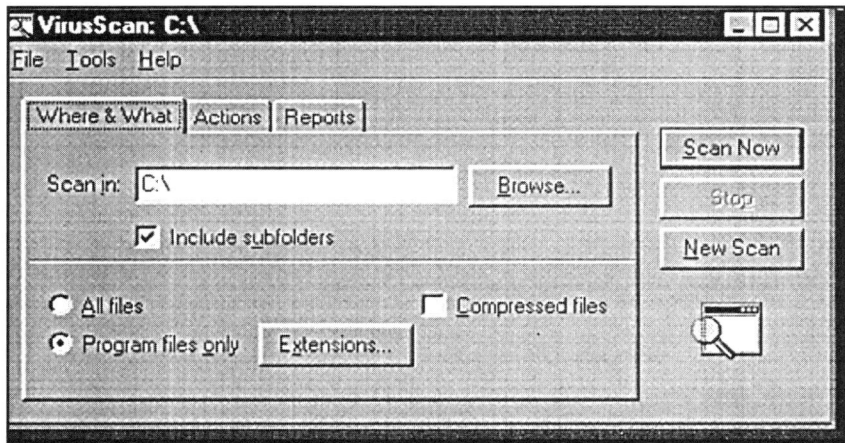

Figure 3.3: Although Virus Scan does a good job of detecting and removing viruses automatically once installed, users can also force the program to scan suspected files, directories or disks at any time.

of my students (I'm the academic advisor to my college's computer club and members come across computer viruses on a regular basis both from data disks used for assignments in our on-campus academic computer labs and, to a lesser extent, from files downloaded over the Internet.) Virus Scan had no difficulty detecting and removing each virus.

Unless you are already using a virus detection program that you trust, by all means get an evaluation copy of Virus Scan as soon as possible. You'll find much to like in this exceptional program to justify its $65 registration fee. The alternative is to continue playing Russian Roulette with your data and programs; no matter how lucky you are, if you keep doing it long enough, a painful, traumatic, potentially fatal consequence will eventually ensue.

Program Name:	Virus Scan® Version 3.12 © 1994-1997
Program Type:	Commercial Software Demo (30 day evaluation)
Company Name:	McAfee Associates, Inc.
Company Address:	McAfee Software
	2805 Bowers Avenue
	Santa Clara, CA 95051-9727
Telephone:	(408) 988-3832
Web Page:	http://www.mcafee.com
Registration Fee:	$65 (Contact McAfee for multiple license pricing.)

General Evaluation: Virus Scan 3.12

	Excellent	*Good*	*Average*	*Poor*
Utility	***			
Ease of Use	***			
Ease of Learning	***			
Documentation	***			
Overall Rating	***			

Norton AntiVirus® Version 4.0

Symantec Corporation's Norton AntiVirus program is an exceptional virus detection, inoculation and removal program from one of the most trusted names in the field. Although this is a commercial package, I've chosen to feature it here because a free, fully functional evaluation version of the program is available for free download and evaluation from the usual shareware distribution sources as well as directly from Symantec (http://www.symantec.com).

Norton AntiVirus works largely unattended once you configure the program to best meet your needs. Once installed, the program automatically searches for boot record viruses at boot up, checks programs for viruses every time you use them, scans files downloaded from the Internet, and scans the startup drive for viruses every week. In addition, the program can be configured to scan specific files, folders or drives at any

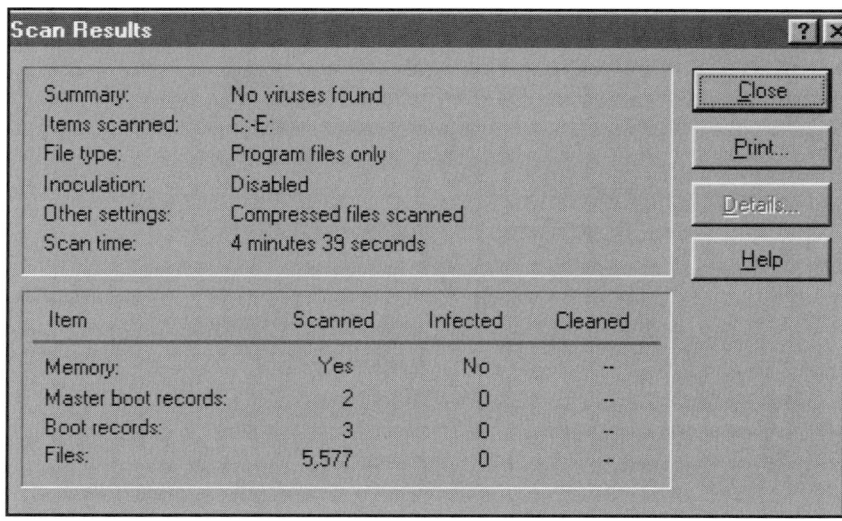

Figure 3.4: *Norton AntiVirus can perform a comprehensive scan of each file in all of your drives (including floppy and removable drives) relatively quickly. Here, the program scanned through nearly three gigabytes of data in three of my logical drives in less than five minutes.*

time, as well as run customized viral scans at predetermined times on a recurring basis. You could, for example, have AntiVirus scan your boot disk and removable disks every day, your program directories every week, and every disk and directory on your system once a month for a comprehensive sweep of your system. The program can also automatically download new virus definitions directly from Symantec's web page every month to keep your program fully updated and capable of detecting and removing the newest viruses.

I have been using the Norton AntiVirus program at work for several years now and have yet to suffer a virus infection thanks to its having detected and erased dozens of viruses during that time period. (I routinely perform comprehensive virus sweeps when I suspect I might have used an infected disk or downloaded an infected file; yet to date, it has never allowed a virus to slip past its automatic monitoring system.)

After installing the trial version of the software, you can automatically download the latest virus definition database directly from Symantec's web page by clicking on "Live Update" from the program's main menu. As of this writing, the program can detect and protect against 12,255 virus strains. You can then evaluate Norton AntiVirus through a 30 day free trial period before the software expires. After that time, you can pur-

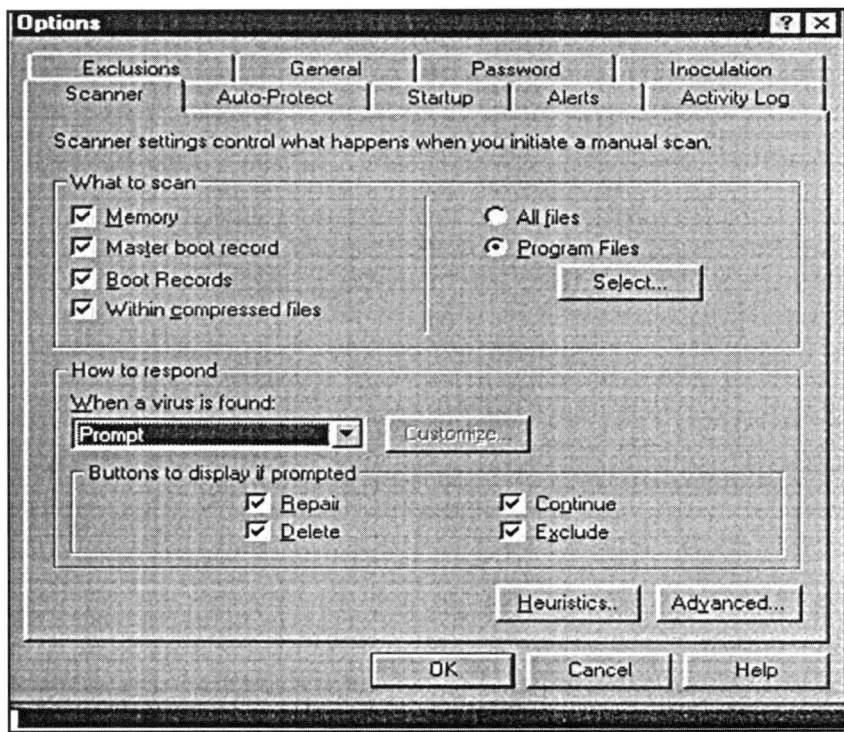

Figure 3.5: *Once installed, you can customize the program in many different ways to meet your specific taste and desired level of protection. The average user will be quite satisfied with the program's default settings which offer very solid protection without unduly slowing down a system's normal operation.*

chase a registered copy from Symantec on-line, or from your favorite software vendor.

Program Name:	Norton AntiVirus® Version 4.0 © 1990-1997
Program Type:	Commercial Software Demo (30 day evaluation)
Company Name:	Symantec Corporation
Company Address:	P.O. Box 599014
	Miami, FL 33159-9963
Web Page:	http://www.symantec.com
Price:	Contact Symantec Corporation or a software retailer for current price. As of this writing, the street price for this product is under $50.

Chapter 3 : Virus Detection and Protection   29

General Evaluation: Norton AntiVirus Version 4.0				
	Excellent	Good	Average	Poor
Utility	***			
Ease of Use	***			
Ease of Learning	***			
Documentation	***			
Overall Rating	***			

ViruSafe 95® Version 2.1

EliaShim's ViruSafe 95 is yet another full featured virus detection and removal program worthy of your attention. ViruSafe is similar in the way that it operates and the protection it offers to both the McAfee and Symantec virus detection products, although it is not as well known as its counterparts.

As is the case with VirusScan and Norton Anti Virus, ViruSafe gives users a wide range of options in the way it can be configured. It can work in the background, scan files downloaded from the Internet for possible viral infections, protect users from viral infection while they surf the Web, and be set up to perform comprehensive scans on a timed basis, such as weekly or monthly. It offers context-sensitive help, though the on-line documentation is less comprehensive than the other two programs reviewed here, and can also directly link to EliaShim's web page for virus downloads—an option only available if you register your copy of the program. Although its virus definition file is somewhat smaller than VirusScan or Norton AntiVirus, this program is by no means a lightweight; this version claims to detect 3942 viruses and 9067 virus mutations.

The program is well integrated, offers an attractive, easy to use interface and should meet the needs of most computer users quite nicely.

Program Name:	ViruSafe 95® Version 2.1 © 1987-1996
Program Type:	Shareware (Unspecified trial period.)
Company Name:	EliaShim, Inc.
Company Address:	1 SW 129th Avenue, Suite 105
	Pembroke Pines, FL 33027
Web Page:	http://www.eliashim.com
E-Mail Address:	support@eliashim.com

Figure 3.6: *EliaShim's ViruSafe offers background virus detection as well as the ability to perform the usual customizable comprehensive scans of all system drives.*

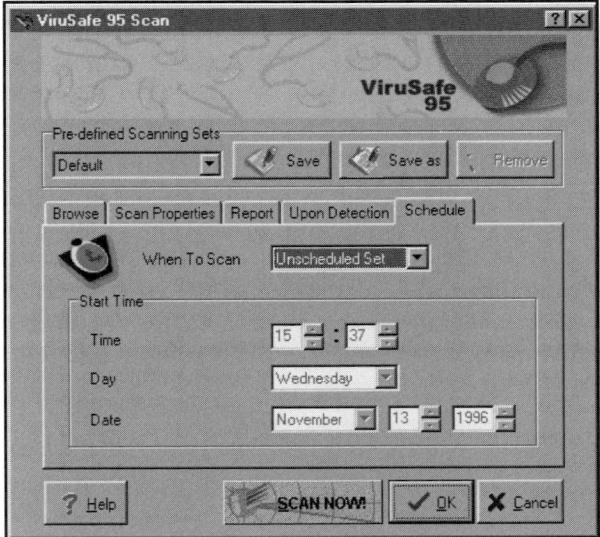

Figure 3.7: *Comprehensive scans of selected files, folders or drives can be automated through the program's scheduling function that is accessible directly from the program's main menu. Scans may be set up once to automatically run hourly, daily, weekly or monthly.*

Registration Fee: $30 for current version (with no updates) or $65 with one year of monthly updates and quarterly upgrades

General Evaluation: VirSafe 95 Version 2.1

	Excellent	*Good*	*Average*	*Poor*
Utility	***			
Ease of Use	***			
Ease of Learning	***			
Documentation			***	
Overall Rating	***			

CHAPTER 4
SYSTEM ANALYSIS

Just how fast is that computer on your desk? How does it compare with other systems in its class? What performance gains have you acquired from that recent memory, processor or video card upgrade? Is your hard disk up to par? These and similar questions can be answered both quickly and accurately with a good system analysis program that can give you accurate, useful performance information about your system that you can then use to fine tune its performance by upgrading components that are not up to par.

Wintune 98® Release 1.0.15

Windows Magazine has a winning freeware program in its and Wintune 98 benchmark analysis utility programs. Both programs provide detailed information about major system components on PC's running Windows 95/98 or Windows NT. The program runs only on computers equipped with Pentium-class processors.

Once installed and run, the program tests basic system components including the CPU, memory, video and hard disks. Once the tests are completed, a process that will take several minutes, the program outputs the test results to the screen and to a data file (see Figure 4.1). This detailed information can then be used to pinpoint weaknesses in your system as well as to gage its relative efficiency and speed.

The current version of the program can be downloaded directly from Windows Magazine's web page (http://www.winmag.com) or run directly

Chapter 4 : System Analysis

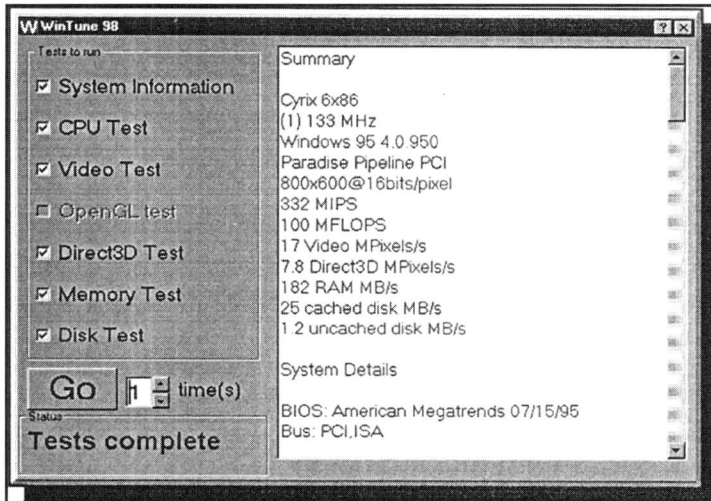

Figure 4.1: Wintune 98 screen showing only a portion of the system information that is provided when the program is run.

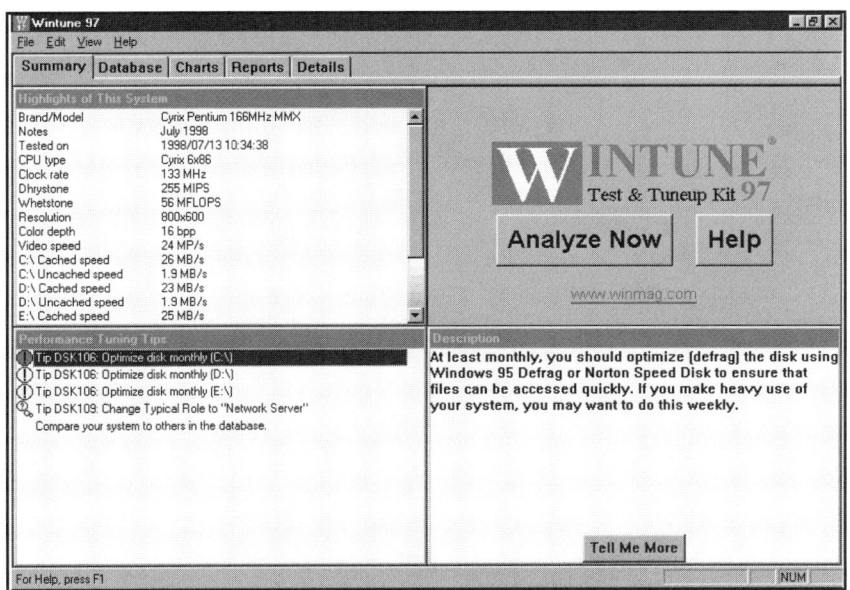

Figure 4.2: Wintune 97 provides the same information as WinTune 98 with a twist: helpful hints on speeding up your system, context sensitive help and a useful database of test results from other computer systems with various hardware configurations that allow you to do side-by-side comparisons of your system's test results.

34   Unit I : Utility Programs

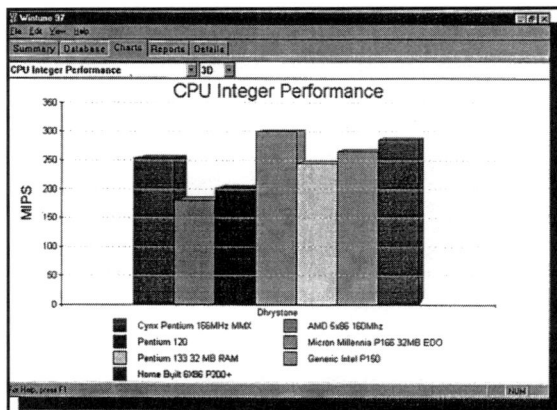

Figure 4.3: See how your system stacks up against computers with similar or different hardware configurations.

while on-line. The program is also readily available from many sites that offer shareware and freeware downloads.

Experienced users will like the no-nonsense user interface and clean data output about their systems. For less experienced users for whom the numbers will mean little by themselves, I recommend the previous version of this program, Wintune 97 Version 1.0, which provides the same information as the latest version with a twist: the ability to do side-by-side comparisons of test data from a user's computer and other computers in a wide variety of configurations. I frankly much prefer Wintune 97 and particularly like the charts it generates, allowing a user to evaluate comparative test results at-a-glance. The database of test results can also be imported into most spreadsheet packages for users who want to further refine the comparative output or generate customized charts.

Whether you prefer the streamlined output of Wintune 98 or the comparative analysis features of Wintune 97, you should find the detailed information both programs provide about your system's performance extremely useful.

Program Name:	Wintune 98® Version 1.0.15 © 1998
	Wintune 97® Version 1.0 © 1997
Program Type:	Freeware
Company Name:	Windows Magazine
Web Page:	http://www.winmag.com
Registration Fee:	None.

General Evaluation: Wintune 98

	Excellent	Good	Average	Poor
Utility	***			
Ease of Use	***			
Ease of Learning	***			
Documentation		***		
Overall Rating	***			

General Evaluation: Wintune 97

	Excellent	Good	Average	Poor
Utility	***			
Ease of Use	***			
Ease of Learning	***			
Documentation	***			
Overall Rating	***			

CHAPTER 5

DISK UTILITIES

Freeware and Shareware utilities to help you diagnose and repair hard disk problems, organize files and otherwise manage your available disk space abound. These can be used to supplement or extend the Windows 95/98 disk utilities (Backup, Disk Defragmenter, DriveSpace and ScanDisk) to help you better manage and maintain applications programs and the data files they generate with their ravenous appetite for disk space.

DiveSpaceCheck® Version 2.0.0

Bill Reid's DriveSpaceCheck is a program that displays the amount of free space on all of your hard disk drives (physical and logical) in a small window anywhere on your screen. You can select to have the window remain always on top of your current open window (see Figure 5.1), or you can close the program after viewing the available disk space on your drives.

This is a nifty small application that can be of value if you frequently download large files from the Internet or if you simply deal with large file transfers on a regular basis. The program even reports the space on removable drives (e.g., Iomega, Syquest and similar varieties), which is helpful if you use these for backup purposes.

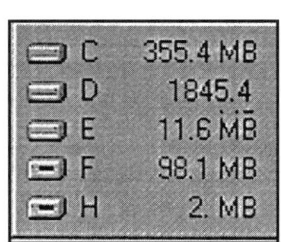

Figure 5.1: A small window lists the available space in all your hard drives.

Program Name:	DriveSpaceCheck® Version 2.0 for Windows 95 © 1994, 1997
Program Type:	Freeware
Programmer:	Bill Reid
E-Mail:	breid@ebicom.net
Web Page:	http://www.ebicom.net/~breid/pfd.htm
Registration Fee:	None for non-commercial use. $5 registration fee for commercial use.

General Evaluation: DriveSpaceCheck Version 2.0

	Excellent	Good	Average	Poor
Utility		***		
Ease of Use	***			
Ease of Learning	***			
Documentation			***	
Overall Rating		***		

Duplication Factory® Version 1.5

Anyone who has ever tried to make multiple copies of floppy disks using Windows 95 will readily attest to the unpleasantness of the task. Windows asks for the original disk at the end of every disk copy, which wastes about a minute of time between the read process and the need to re-insert the source disk (the disk to be copied). This is a minor inconvenience to most users who seldom need to duplicate floppy disks, but can be a real headache for the small number of users who regularly duplicate multiple copies of disks for data backup, data or software distribution or educational purposes. Fortunately, there is an elegant, low cost solution to the problem: the Duplication Factory.

The Duplication Factory obviates the need to re-insert the source disk after each copy operation by creating an image of the disk that can be held in RAM to allow as many copies of the disk to be made as are needed. In addition, for disks that may need to be copied more than once, the disk image can be saved on the hard disk and accessed by the program at a later time—an operation that is significantly faster than re-reading the disk through the computer's slower floppy disk drive. The program can verify the integrity of the data copied to duplicate disks, thus insuring that the copied disks are identical to the original, a feature not available for disks duplicated through Windows 95.

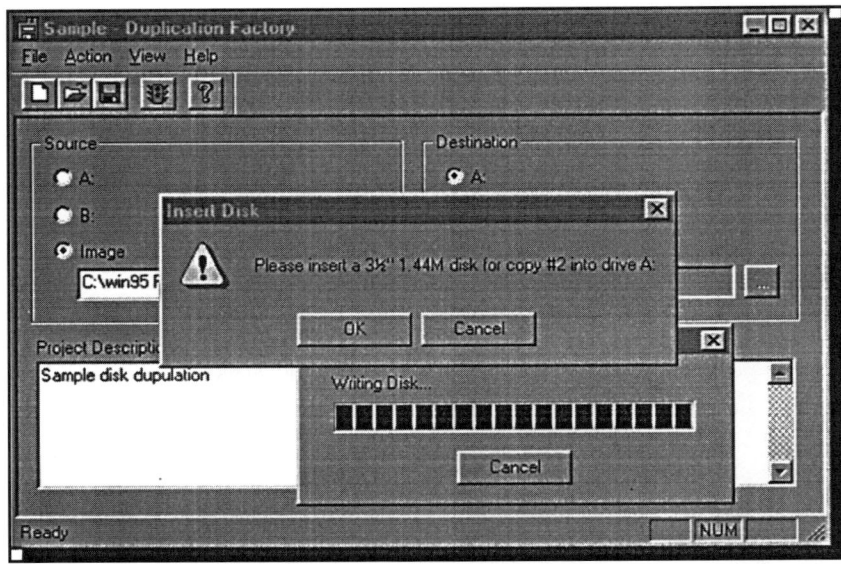

Figure 5.2: Duplication Factory Version 1.5. Multiple copies of floppy disks can be made by either reading the source disk once or by loading a copy of a previously saved disk image from your hard disk. Automatic formatting of disks and data verification are also supported.

By using the Duplication Factory, the time it takes to make multiple copies of a floppy disk is cut in half (approximately one minute per disk rather than the two minutes it takes using Windows 95). The demo version of the program limits the user to making not more than three copies from any one disk, but is otherwise the same as the full commercial version. Users who need to make multiple copies of floppy disks regularly will find this program saves them both time and the frustration of unnecessary disk swaps.

Program Name:	Duplication Factory® Version 1.5 ©1997
Program Type:	Demo Version (May evaluate for 30 days but must register if continue to use thereafter. Limited to 3 copies per disk image.)
Company:	Indigo Rose Corporation
Address:	PO Box 2159
	Winnipeg MB, Canada R3C 3R5
Phone:	(204) 946-0263
Fax:	(204) 942-3421

E-mail: support@indigorose.com
Web Page: http://www.indigorose.com
Registration Fee: $29.95

General Evaluation: Duplication Factory Version 1.5

	Excellent	Good	Average	Poor
Utility		***		
Ease of Use	***			
Ease of Learning	***			
Documentation			***	
Overall Rating			***	

TidyDisk® Version 1.0

Both Windows 95/98 and the programs run under these operating systems create a wide range of temporary files during their normal operation. Such files are necessary to speed up the way that applications run and to protect against data loss when the inevitable Windows crash occurs. In theory, most temporary files are automatically erased when Windows or the applications programs that create them are shut down normally. In reality, many such files are never erased due to improper system shutdowns, such as software or hardware glitches that cause a system to crash; this prevents the normal erasure of all open temporary files the program was using before crashing, and results in temporary files being left behind, cluttering already bloated drives with the electronic flotsam and jetsam of crashed programs.

You can, of course, manually remove such files, if you know where they reside. Some, such as Windows cache and temp files, are easy to find. Others, such as the temporary files that programs create and save under various directories, are much harder to find. TidyDisk makes the process simple by automatically combing all directories in the drives you specify for a wide range of common temporary files. When it finds such files, a process that takes less than a minute on a typical system, it gives you a wide range of options on dealing with such files including deleting some or all of them, archiving them in a ZIP file to save disk space, or sending them all to a specific directory where they can be later examined. The program even allows a variety of options as to how selected files can be deleted; these include sending files to the recycle bin, deleting such files

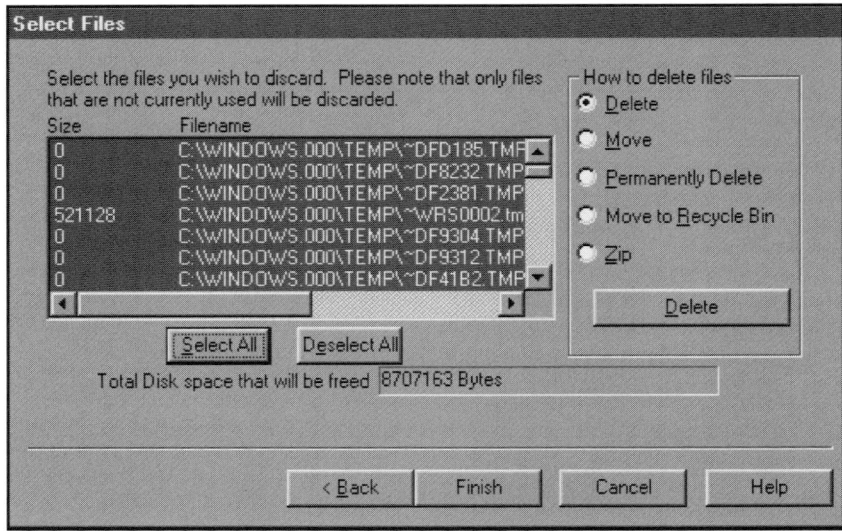

Figure 5.3: TidyDisk automatically flags temporary files currently on your system and gives you a variety of options for dealing with them either individually or as a group. It took less than 30 seconds to find nearly nine megabytes of temporary files across six physical and logical hard disk drives.

(an option that yields the same effect as deleting files through Windows Explorer) or permanently deleting the files (an option that renders them unrecoverable in the future). As a safety feature, it will not delete any files that are currently in use by Windows or any program, thus preventing accidental file deletions that might cause currently running programs to crash and data to be lost.

TidyDisk offers brief but useful on-line documentation that will have both novice and experienced users comfortably using the program with ease. It is a simple, useful, quick that will painlessly trim the unnecessary fat from your hard disk.

Program Name:	TidyDisk® Version 1.0 ©1997
Program Type:	Shareware (May evaluate for 30 days but must register if continue to use thereafter.)
Company:	American Systems
Address:	5424 Rufe Snow #320
	Fort Worth, TX 76180
Phone:	1-888-892-4310

Fax: (817) 485-2193
E-mail: support@americansys.com
Web Page: http://www.americansys.com
Registration Fee: $19.95

General Evaluation: TidyDisk Version 1.0

	Excellent	Good	Average	Poor
Utility	***			
Ease of Use	***			
Ease of Learning	***			
Documentation			***	
Overall Rating	***			

LifeSaver® Version 3.30

LifeSaver is a configuration file backup and restore utility that can be used to recover from problems related to corrupt or accidentally altered configuration files. The program permits up to seven configuration files to be backed up and replaced, and allows system files to be restored from the DOS command prompt in case of a failure that prevents Windows from loading properly. The registered version of the program allows additional features that include automated timed backups of up to ten configuration files and optional compression / decompression of file backups. These additional features are available on the shareware version of the program for 30 days but are disabled thereafter. The main program features, however, are not disabled once the trial period expires.

In its default configuration, LifeSaver automatically backs up the following system files: system.dat, user.dat, protocol.ini, system.ini, win.ini, autoexec.bat and config.sys. If added to the start folder, the registered version of the program can be scheduled to automatically back up these files every time your system is started, or on a daily or weekly basis. The program can also automatically schedule backups based on a user-selected number of days (e.g., every 15 or 30 days).

LifeSaver includes an intuitive interface and solid on-line documentation. The process of backing up vital system files takes less than a minute and can save you many hours reconstructing or reinstalling corrupted, erased or rewritten files when the inevitable happens. Of course, you can achieve the same basic function for this program by writing a simple DOS batch file to copy critical files to a backup directory at every boot up, but

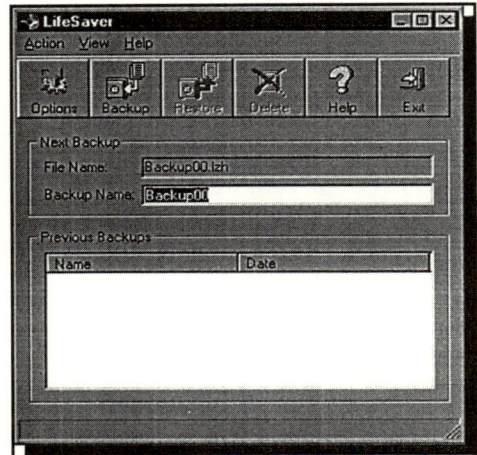

Figure 5.4: LiveSaver 3.30.

this program makes the process foolproof for new users and provides some additional features even experienced users will find useful.

Program Name:	LifeSaver® Version 3.30 ©1995-1997 Jeffrey A. Becker
Program Type:	Shareware (Registration is not required, although some features are disabled after 30 days of use.)
Company:	JB Systems
Address:	4880-8 Dorsey Hall Dr. Ellicott City, MD 21042
Phone:	(914) 354-8666
E-mail:	Aeroblade@aol.com
Registration Fee:	$18.00 to register the freeware version $29.95 to receive retail version that includes the program on floppy disks.

General Evaluation: LifeSaver Version 3.30

	Excellent	Good	Average	Poor
Utility		***		
Ease of Use		***		
Ease of Learning		***		
Documentation		***		
Overall Rating		***		

CHAPTER 6
FILE UTILITIES

Windows 95/98 provides useful built-in file manipulation capabilities, including the ability to erase and copy files, as well as move files between disks or directories. The programs reviewed in this chapter significantly enhance those capabilities and should prove useful to most Windows users.

BCWipe®

Many Windows users are unaware that files deleted through Windows 95/98 or through Windows programs can easily be recovered by using one of many disk utility programs such as Norton Utilities. This is true even of programs that have been sent to the recycle bin once the recycle bin is emptied, or of programs deleted through DOS and data held in temporary storage such as cache files or the Windows swap file. Thus, whenever sensitive data is accessed, the possibility exists for that data to be recovered by nearly any computer user who has access to that system and possesses some basic computer skills. Sensitive data should never be casually erased, especially when a freeware programs such as BCWipe makes the process of shredding electronic data quick, simple, effective and free.

Once installed, BCWipe can be accessed directly from Windows Explorer by right clicking your mouse after a file or files have been selected for deletion. The program allows you to select from simple (two-pass delete and wipe) or Department of Defense approved (seven-pass delete and wipe) options. The program also allows the windows swap file to be wiped to prevent sensitive information from being recovered from it.

Unit I : Utility Programs

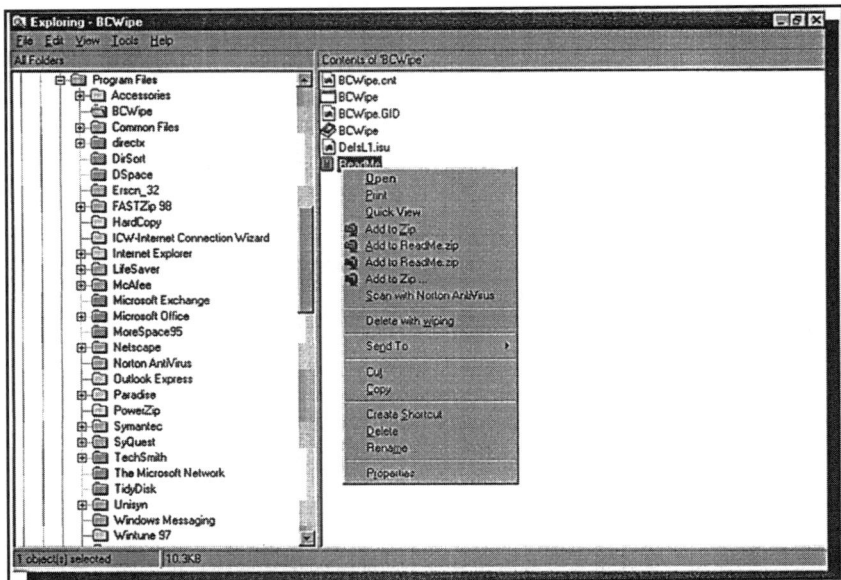

Figure 6.1: *Once installed, BCWipe allows you to easily delete files from Windows Explorer by right clicking on selected files and choosing the "Delete with Wiping" option from the quick menu.*

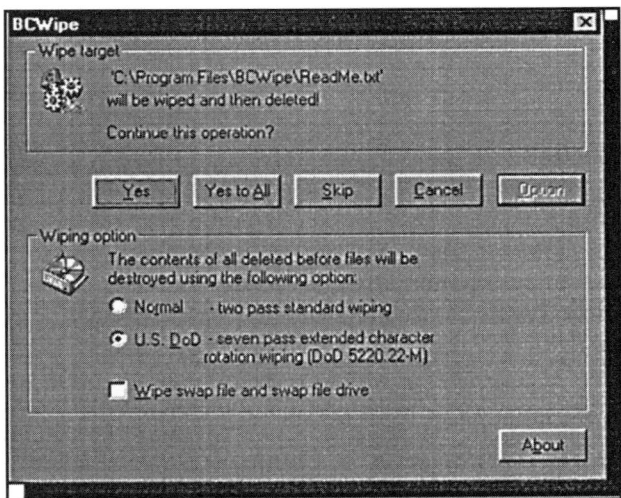

Figure 6.2: *Choose from Normal or Department of Defense approved file shredding. You may also elect to wipe the Windows swap file for additional protection against illicit recovery of sensitive data.*

Program Name:	BCWipe® ©1993-1997
Program Type:	Freeware
Company:	Jetico, Inc.
Web Page:	http://www.jetico.sci.fi
E-mail:	jetico@sci.fi
Registration Fee:	None

General Evaluation: BCWipe

	Excellent	Good	Average	Poor
Utility	***			
Ease of Use	***			
Ease of Learning		***		
Documentation		***		
Overall Rating		***		

Syncer!® Version 1.1

Syncer! is a simple, no-nonsense file synchronization program that allows you to ensure that files and directories on two separate disks will be identical. It is a very useful program for users who keep backup directories of crucial data or programs on separate drives or on separate directories on a single drive. When invoked, the program allows you to automatically synchronize the contents of selected directories, making them identical. When identical files are found, the program automatically copies the latest version of the file from one drive or directory to the other, thus ensuring that selected drives or directories contain true mirror images of one another with only the latest versions of files.

Read-only files can optionally be updated if a later copy of the same file exists in a directory being synchronized; if the user so chooses, the read-only attribute is automatically removed, the newer file version copied over the read-only file, and the attribute then replaced once the update is complete. According to the author, the program may encounter problems with sharing violations if synchronized files are open on target drives of directories when the program is run. It is therefore a good idea to run the program with no unnecessary files open in directories or drives being synchronized—a minor inconvenience given the program's fast execution.

Although the program contains little by way of documentation, it is very simple to use. Unlike some other similar programs, it does not allow automatic synchronization of selected drives or directories; the program

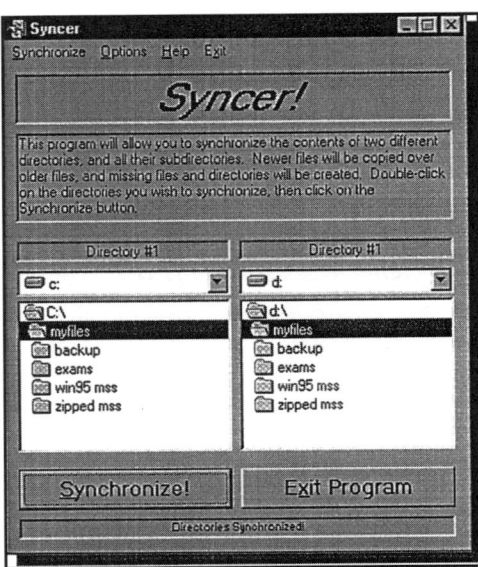

Figure 6.3: After selecting and synchronizing target drives and directories, Syncer! copies all necessary files and subdirectories from one drive to another, ensuring a perfect mirror image of the selected directory or directories that contain only the latest version of files.

must manually be run every time a user wants to synchronize files. Unlike more feature packed programs, however, this freeware utility requires no registration and does what it is intended to do quite nicely.

Program Name:	Syncer!® Version 1.1 ©1996
Program Type:	Freeware
Programmer:	Tony Fodera
E-mail:	flame@gte.net
Registration Fee:	None

General Evaluation: Syncer! Version 1.1

	Excellent	Good	Average	Poor
Utility		***		
Ease of Use	***			
Ease of Learning	***			
Documentation			***	
Overall Rating		***		

Splitit95® Version 1.0

Computer programs have grown steadily larger over the past 20 years to the point that it has made the venerable floppy disk all but obsolete as a means of software distribution. And where software has gone, data files are quickly following. Even lowly word processing, spreadsheet and database files, the staples of every business computer user, have developed voracious appetites for disk space as we cram even simple documents with high-resolution color graphics, scanned images, and charts, wantonly experiment with (and overuse) the nifty fonts in our word processor's arsenal, and annotate our documents with voice messages and video clips. The simple book you're holding is a good case in point: the first four books I've published to date all fit (barely) on a single 1.44 MB floppy disk. The first draft of this book up to this point requires more than 16 Megabytes of disk space due almost exclusively to the high resolution captured screen illustrations it includes—nearly ten times more disk space than my 456-page *Legal Environment of Business* textbook!. And the first draft of Unit 5 requires more than 90 MB or storage space for 94 pages of text and

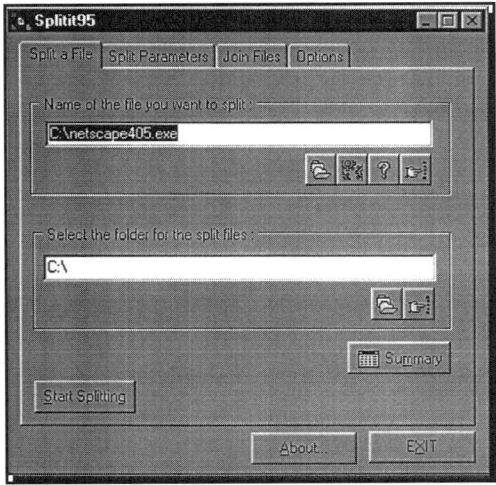

Figure 6.4: *The process of splitting a large file into several smaller ones with Splitit95 requires a user to select the file to be split and a directory to send the copies of the file to. It also requires a user to select exactly how files are split, a process illustrated in Figure 6.5. In this test run, I asked the program to split the 10.5 megabyte distribution file of my Netscape Navigator program so that it would fit into 1.4 MB disks. The program dutifully complied, giving me seven smaller sequentially-numbered files that could be placed on the requested floppy disk size.*

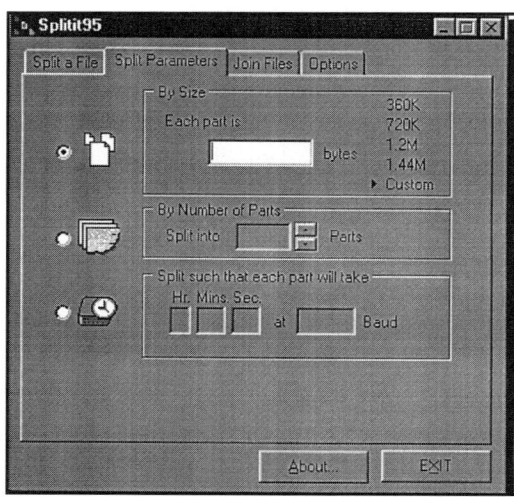

Figure 6.5: Once a file is identified for splitting and the target directory chosen for saving the new split files, you must tell the program how to split up the files. Options include selecting a set number of equal files, selecting the type of disk size into which the files will be copied later, or choosing the amount of time at a given baud rate that each new file should take when transmitted.

graphics. How, then, do you transfer such large files given the storage limitations of the ubiquitous floppy disk? Two options that quickly come to mind are backup and file compression programs. You can back up very large files or entire disks using either a stand-alone backup program or Windows' own backup program. You can also stuff space-hungry graphics, video and sound files into a space as small as 10% of their original size by using one of the compression programs reviewed in Chapter 1. But sometimes these programs are not the best alternatives. For instance, a 10-megabyte ZIP file won't fit on a floppy disk, and files backed up by a backup utility require the same utility be available when they are to be restored. Fortunately, lesser known third alternative is available: programs that split up a large file into smaller segments that can be saved on disk for easy transfer to another system then re-assembled when copied to their new location. Such is the function of Splitit95 and a host of similar programs.

Splitting large files with Splitit95 requires a few steps, but the process is by no means cumbersome. First, the name of the file to be split must be selected, followed by the directory to which the split files will be saved. The program must then be told how many new files to split the original file into; the user can select any number of equal-sized files (e.g., if a three megabyte file is to be split, you can select to split it into two 1.5 megabyte files, three one- megabyte files, ten 300 kilobyte files, or any other equal-sized number of files you choose). You can also tell the program the size of disks the files will be copied onto, and the program will then automatically divide the file so that it fits on such disks, or you can even divide the file into a length that is geared towards modem transmission (e.g., split the file into chunks that can be transmitted in ten minutes over your modem's particular transmission baud rate) When splitting files, the program will use, by default, the name of the original file with a different numbered extension for each split file; that makes keeping track of split files a simple process.

Unifying the split files requires a reversal of the process. By selecting the first split file, the program automatically sews together the remaining files in the series to comprise a single file that is the same as the original. You need only tell it what directory to save the combined new file to. It should be noted here that the original file is not physically removed from your drive or altered at any time but remains intact in its original location.

If you use Splitit95 to transfer large files to other people, you must also give them a copy of the program. Fortunately, the program is freeware and fits on a single floppy disk, so you can share both it and your large data files with anyone you like.

Program Name: Splitit95® Version 1.0 ©1996
Program Type: Freeware
Programmer: Kevin Arouza
E-mail: kevarouza@poboxes.com
Registration Fee: None

General Evaluation: Splitit95 Version 1.0

	Excellent	Good	Average	Poor
Utility	***			
Ease of Use	***			
Ease of Learning	***			
Documentation			***	
Overall Rating	***			

Chgname® Version 4.0

Chgname Version 4.0 is a powerful file utility program that gives users great flexibility in changing file names, date stamps and file attributes. The program can work with files one at a time or in groups selected by a user and has the ability to simultaneously rename and copy or move selected files to different target directories.

This specialized utility will perhaps prove most useful to persons who work with large numbers of related files that do not have similar filenames, such as graphics files downloaded from the Internet. For example, let's suppose you download high resolution images of travel locations and have amassed hundreds of JPG images of France, Italy, Germany and Spain with a variety of file names that are not necessarily descriptive (e.g., country.jpg, man.jpg, fisherman.jpg, beach.jpg, cityscape.jpg, and so on). Using Chgname, you can select all images from an individual country and then have the program selectively rename them so that they are sequentially numbered and share a common file name (e.g., germany001.jpg,

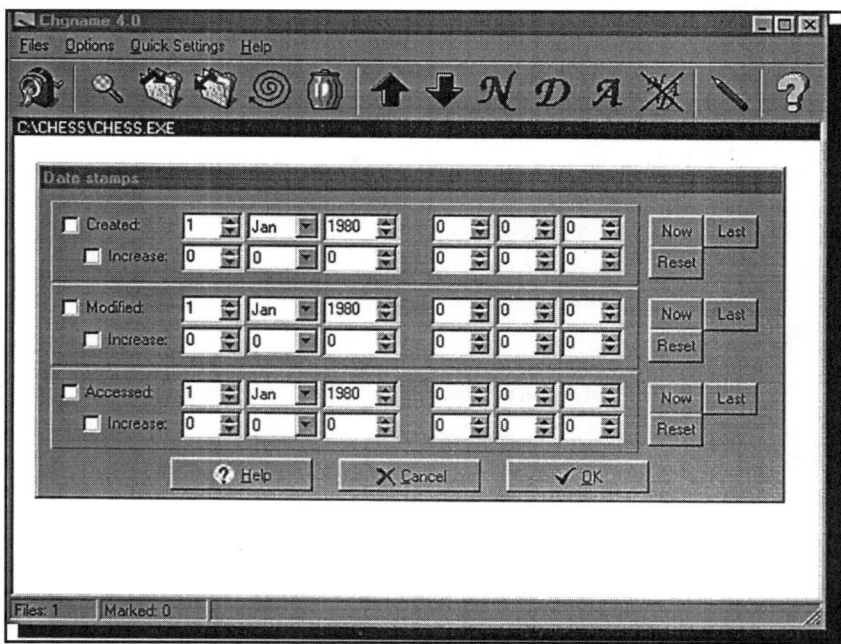

Figure 6.6: Chgname provides great flexibility in changing not only file names and attributes, but also the date stamp relating to the file's creation, modification or access, as seen here.

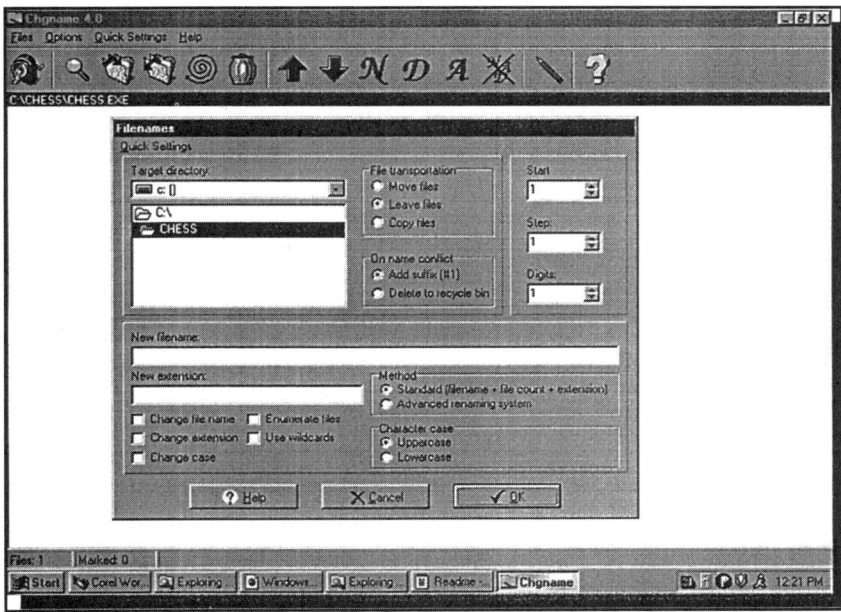

Figure 6.7: Changing the name of a single file (as in this example) or sequentially renaming thousands of related files while simultaneously moving or copying them to different drives or directories can be accomplished with ease, once a user becomes familiar with the program's documentation. Chgname provides a great deal of flexibility and power that will be welcomed especially by users who wish to better organize and customize large numbers of files.

germany002.jpg, and so on). You can simultaneously change the file creation date and time of each file so that it reflects not necessarily the date and time it was actually created, but rather the date and time you copied the file, traveled to the location or snapped the subsequently scanned photograph. The program can process name, attribute, time and date changes for up to 32,767 files at once.

Because it offers users great flexibility, Chgname is not one of the easiest Windows 95/98 programs to use. The program requires a user to spend some time reading the on-line documentation carefully before attempting to use the program. Given that this utility is likeliest to be used by experienced users, the learning curve for this program does not represent a real problem, especially given the generally solid documentation accessible through the program's help menu. (Despite occasional lapses in grammar and spelling, the documentation and context-sensitive help are far superior to that of many commercial packages.)

Program Name:	Chgname® Version 4.0 ©1997
Program Type:	Freeware
Programmer:	Kjetil L. Nygård
Web Page:	http://www.uio.no/~kln/
E-mail:	k.l.nygard@hfstud.uio.no
Registration Fee:	None

General Evaluation: Chgname Version 4.0

	Excellent	Good	Average	Poor
Utility	***			
Ease of Use	***			
Ease of Learning			***	
Documentation			***	
Overall Rating	***			

Calypso® Version 1.0

Calypso is a utility program intended to replace Windows Explorer. The program offers the same basic file management features as Explorer with some additional useful utilities built-in. Among its many enhancements are the ability to print a file directly from the program shell either through Windows or through the file's native program, greater flexibility in sorting files on screen, the ability to change not just file names and attributes but also file dates and time stamps, direct support for ZIP file compression and decompression, and support for text-string searches within tagged files.

In addition to offering more powerful file utilities than Explorer, Calypso provides additional useful information about directories, disks and tagged files, including information about the local disk's total and available space, and the size of the active directory and all its subdirectories as well as the total number of files they contain. Calypso also allows direct access to some useful Windows accessory programs and features directly from its tools menu, including the Windows Calculator, System Monitor, Registry Editor and Control Panel.

In short, Calypso offers users the basic flexibility of Explorer with some additional features most users will find useful. The learning curve for this program is minimal because of its similar look and feel to Explorer, and the fact that it can be customized to work for all intents and purposes as an Explorer clone. On the down side, the program carries a relatively

Chapter 6 : File Utilities

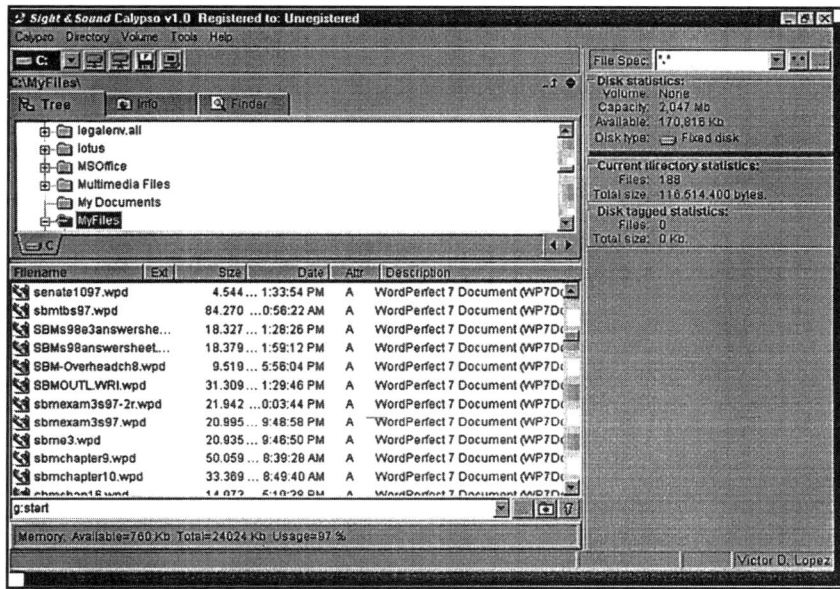

Figure 6.8: Calypso offers a Windows Explorer-like interface with some notable improvements, including better disk and directory information, more sorting options, built-in ZIP file compression and decompression support and direct access to some commonly used Windows features.

hefty registration fee of $59.95 and the Shareware version pops up an annoying registration reminder on a periodic basis as you evaluate the program—two factors that caused me to downgrade its overall score by ten points.

Program Name:	Calypso® Version 1.0 ©1997
Program Type:	Shareware (30 day free trial. After 30 day trial period, must register or uninstall the program.)
Company:	Sight & Sound
Address:	Kamniska g. 11
	SI-2351 Kamniska
	Slovenia
Web Page:	http://www.sight-sound.si
Registration Fee:	$59.95

General Evaluation: Calypso Version 1.0

	Excellent	Good	Average	Poor
Utility		***		
Ease of Use	***			
Ease of Learning	***			
Documentation	***			
Overall Rating		***		

CHAPTER 7
MOUSE UTILITIES

Novel and quite useful pointing devices abound, yet none will likely soon replace the humble mouse as the typical Windows user's favorite means of getting around the computer screen. While we await the invention of the better mouse, there are a number of utilities currently available that can teach your old rodent some new tricks. In this chapter we'll sample a few of the more interesting ones.

MousePad® Version 1.0

MousePad is a simple utility program that allows a mouse to be used to type text as an alternative to a standard keyboard. The program is of particular interest to users who might find it easier to work with a mouse or compatible pointing device rather than a traditional keyboard due to physical limitations.

Once installed and run, the program pops up a small QUERY virtual keyboard on your monitor and allows you to "type in" letters by clicking on the virtual keyboard's keys. A CapsLock key is available for typing all uppercase text. To type a single uppercase letter, the Shift key is clicked on followed by the letter to be capitalized.

Typed text can be copied to the clipboard in a single step by clicking on the program's Copy button. Once copied, keyed text can be pasted onto any other application in the traditional method.

As you might expect, typing with a mouse is a relatively slow process when compared to using a traditional keyboard, but for persons with limited mobility for whom a standard keyboard might be harder to use than

56   Unit I : Utility Programs

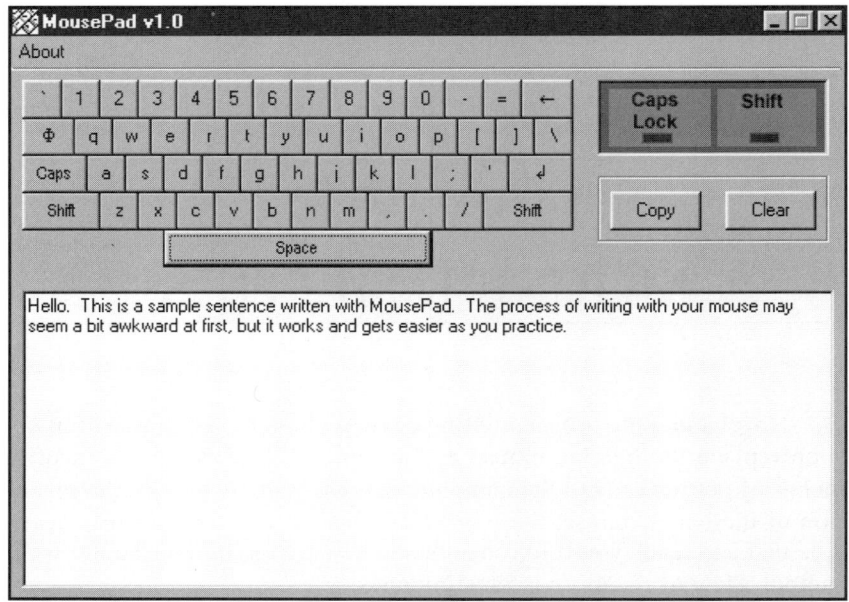

Figure 7.1: MousePad Version 1.0

a mouse, the program offers a workable means of entering text into nearly any application program.

Program Name:	MousePad® Version 1.0 ©1997
Program Type:	Freeware
Company:	Interrupt Infinity
Address:	P.O. Box 457
	West Chester, OH 45071
Web Page:	http://www.interruptinfinity.com
E-Mail:	Jason.Ertel@interruptinfinity.com
Registration Fee:	None

General Evaluation: MousePad Version 1.0

	Excellent	Good	Average	Poor
Utility		***		
Ease of Use	***			
Ease of Learning	***			
Documentation		***		
Overall Rating		***		

Pointix® Version 2.60

Pointix Version 2.60 is a remarkably useful utility program that significantly extends the capability of your mouse.

In a nutshell, this program allows the normal left and right mouse buttons to be supplemented by four additional "virtual buttons" that can be accessed through some simple mouse movements. Once loaded, the program allows a customizable menu to pop up whenever four distinct mouse motions are executed by the user: a clockwise circle, a counter-clockwise circle, a quick left-right motion and a quick up-down motion. Moving the mouse in a quick clockwise circle pops up an utilities window that gives the user access to some useful included programs that include a scheduler, reminder program, calculator, memo and cardfile, along with immediate access to your favorite Windows utilities and programs (see Figure 7.2). Moving the mouse in a quick counterclockwise circle pops up a General Floatbar menu with customizable commands that relate to the program running in your active window (e.g., open and close files, switch windows, perform cut and paste operations, and so on). A quick left-right mouse motion pops up a Favorite Shortcuts menu that gives you quick, customizable access to, among other things, your favorite applications, your start menu, all desktop shortcuts and your most recently opened files. Finally, a quick up-down mouse motion allows you to switch between all currently open programs.

In addition to the four additional motion-sensitive functions assigned

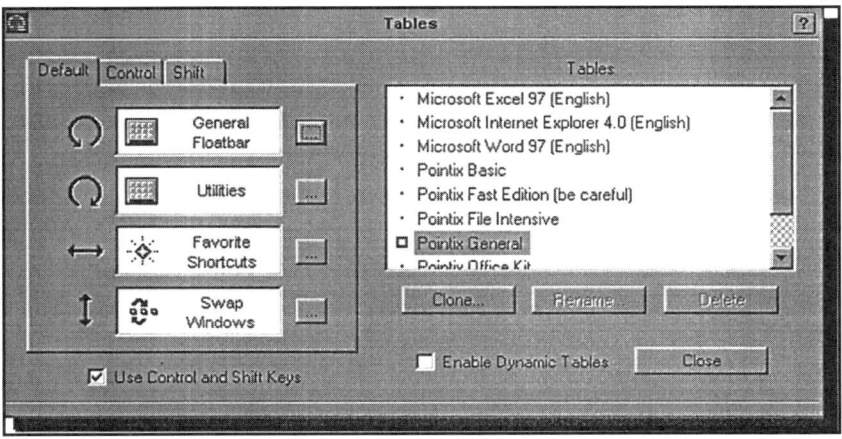

Figure 7.2: Pointix Version 2.60 allows you open useful customizable menus by performing certain mouse movements within Windows or any application program.

to your mouse by the program, Pointix allows you to quickly and naturally scroll through any open document by holding down the right mouse button and then moving the mouse in the direction you wish to scroll. Vertical and horizontal scrolling may be carried out simultaneously in this way without the need to click on the respective scroll bars—and with much greater control. (Tapping on the right mouse button will still allow you to access the normal quick menus available in Windows and in your favorite application programs.) The program can also be customized to allow access to Shift and Control key sequences so that different functions can be assigned to the motion-sensitive pop-up menus. These can include customized commands for Microsoft Excel, Word, and Explorer. In this way, you could program your favorite Microsoft Excel 97 commands to pop up when you hold the Shift key and execute a quick counter-clock circle motion with your mouse, and your most used Microsoft Word 97 commands to be available when you hold the Control key and execute the same motion.

In all, Pointix is an excellent utility program that teaches your old mouse some very useful new tricks. It is by far the best mouse utility program I have seen.

Program Name: Pointix® Version 2.60 ©1997
Program Type: Shareware / Demo (15-day free trial)
Company: Pointix Corporation
Address: 1373 SW 23rd St.
Miami, FL 33145
Web Page: http://www.pointix.com
E-Mail: support@pointix.com
Registration Fee: Contact Pointix Corporation for current pricing.

General Evaluation: Pointix Version 2.60

	Excellent	*Good*	*Average*	*Poor*
Utility	***			
Ease of Use	***			
Ease of Learning	***			
Documentation	***			
Overall Rating	***			

Cool Mouse® 97 Version 2.1

Cool Mouse 97 increases the usefulness of your mouse by allowing you to assign preprogrammed functions to the third mouse button found on most mice. Even if you have a traditional two-button mouse, this utility can allow it to function as a three-button mouse by treating the right mouse button as a third (middle) mouse button whenever the Scroll Lock key is on.

Available features include the following:

Double-Click (when in use, this feature treats a single click of the middle mouse button as a double-click of the left mouse button);

Pop-up Start Menu (displays the "Start Menu" anywhere on the screen);

Roll Up Window (rolls any window clicked on to its title bar);

Window Features (offers a menu if Windows operations);

Tray Window (allows up to 15 open windows to be minimized to the task bar notification area);

Scroll Window (allows the scrolling of windows without the need to use scroll bars);

Run Program (enables you to run any predefined program with a click of the middle mouse button); and

Drag and Drop (permits objects to be drag and dropped without holding down the left mouse button).

Despite somewhat spotty documentation, the program is relatively easy to learn and use. A bit of experimentation will have the average user comfortable with using the mouse's newfound capabilities in relatively short order, and every user should find one or more of the available features handy for everyday use.

The middle mouse button, much as the IBM-PC compatible A/C female monitor plug that is still sometimes mindlessly replicated by clone makers on their system cases (even IBM monitors have not used that type of power plug in years!), seems to be one of those seemingly good ideas that never quite caught on but is still mindlessly reproduced for the general amusement of computer users everywhere. With Cool Mouse 97, you can gain some useful function from that extra mouse button that software developers have long chosen to ignore.

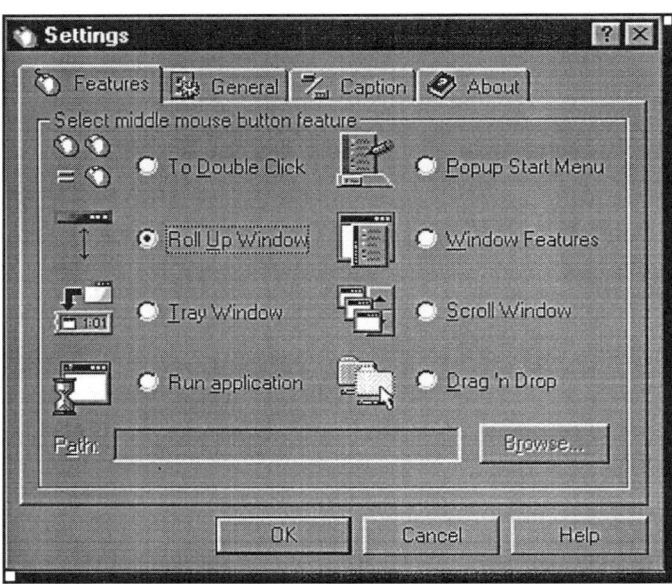

Figure 7.3: *Cool Mouse 97 allows you to assign a variety of functions to the normally unused middle button of your mouse. It can also extend the functions of a two-button mouse by using the Scroll Lock key to toggle dual functions to the right mouse button.*

Program Name: Cool Mouse 97® Version 2.1 ©1997
Program Type: Freeware
Programmer: Kirill M. Kirillov
Web Page: http://www.pointix.com
Registration Fee: None

General Evaluation: Cool Mouse 97 Version 2.1

	Excellent	Good	Average	Poor
Utility		***		
Ease of Use		***		
Ease of Learning		***		
Documentation			***	
Overall Rating		***		

UNIT II
PERSONAL PRODUCTIVITY

A personal computer equipped with the right software can become an excellent personal productivity enhancement tool that can help you better manage your time, your finances and, in general, make your life a little easier. In this unit, well look at a potpourri of Windows 95/98 tools that can assist you with the varied tasks of managing your loans, your printer, your time and your personal information.

CHAPTER 8
LOAN CALCULATORS

Whether it's calculating an amortization schedule on a loan to learn how much principal you still owe after a set number of payments, the monthly payments on your next car, the monthly mortgage payments on a new home, or the maximum value of a home you can currently afford, the following financial programs will provide quick, accurate information that you can use to help better manage your personal finances.

Quick Quote® Version 1.01

Quick Quote is a no-nonsense loan calculator that provides you with loan payment information for any loan. You simply type in the amount of the loan, the interest rate, the number of payments that will be made on the loan and the frequency of payments (e.g., weekly, biweekly, monthly or bimonthly). The program then calculates the exact amount of each payment based on the information provided.

The program does not incorporate an install utility, so that you will need to manually copy it to whatever directory you wish and then either run it from that directory through Windows Explorer or create a shortcut to the program so that you can access it from the desktop. Given that the program decompresses into just two files (the program itself and a license text file) that take up under 300K bytes combined, this is not a real concern. Indeed, you could simply choose to decompress the ZIP file containing the program right onto the root directory of your boot drive and leave it there for easy access when you need it.

Quick Quote is probably the best program to use when you're looking

Unit II : Personal Productivity

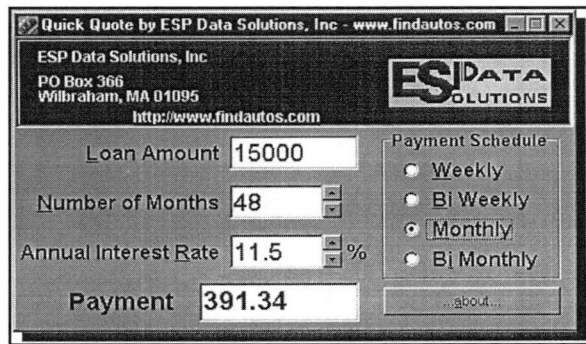

Figure 8.1: Quick Quote allows you to calculate periodic payments for any loan with weekly, biweekly, monthly or bimonthly payment terms. It is a good starting point in evaluating basic financing options for any loan.

for a fast way to calculate periodic payments on a loan. It allows you to do quick "what if" calculations based on different payment terms, and to gauge the affordability of a loan with a minimum of effort. While it does not offer such niceties as loan amortization tables or comparative analysis of the exact cost of financing a loan, often these considerations are non essential for the preliminary stages of evaluating your financing options. In the time it takes to load that custom, full-featured loan amortization spreadsheet file you've created for your Excel or Lotus programs, Quick Quote can give you a half dozen quick answers to the question "What will my monthly payment be on a $15,000 loan to finance my next new car?"

Program Name: Quick Quote® Version 1.01 © 1997
Program Type: Freeware
Company Name: ESP Data Solutions, Inc.
Company Address: P.O. Box 366, Wilbraham, MA 10195
Registration Fee: None

General Evaluation: Quick Quote Version 1.01

	Excellent	Good	Average	Poor
Utility		***		
Ease of Use	***			
Ease of Learning	***			
Documentation				***
Overall Rating		***		

EZ Loan Manager 97® Version 4.20

EZ Loan Manager 97 is an easy to use loan amortization program that allows you to easily prepare a first year loan amortization schedule for any loan. The program allows you to perform a variety of "what if" calculations for any loan, including seeing the interest cost savings of making extra monthly or yearly payments of any amount, and the ability to work backwards to determine the interest rate or term necessary to achieve a specific monthly payment.

The program provides useful statistics for comparing a variety of loan options, including interest costs fort the first year and total interest costs for the life of the loan. Although only the first year's amortization table can be seen on your monitor, the program allows you to print a full

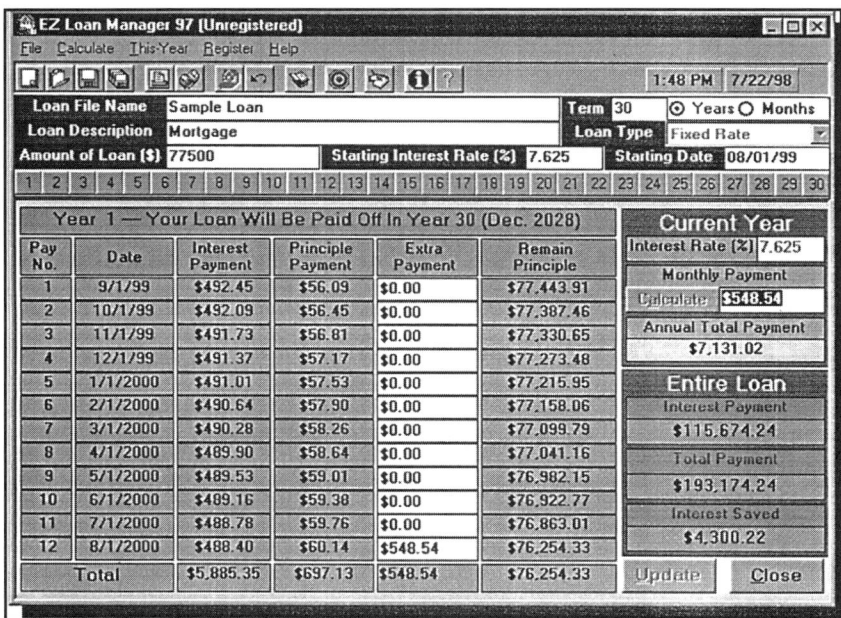

Figure 8.2: EZ Loan Manager 97 allows you to easily create and print customized loan analysis reports that can be saved, printed and compared to help you minimize your credit expenses. The program can not only show you your credit cost for the year and for the entire loan, but also the interest savings that can be realized by making extra payments of any amount during the life of the loan. Shown here on a sample mortgage loan with an extra mortgage payment made on the 12th month of the loan. Note how the $548.54 payment results over the life of the loan in a total savings of $4,300.22.

Unit II : Personal Productivity

Loan Calculator	
Calculate one unknown by giving the interest rate and two other known numbers	
Amount of Loan ($)	12000
Interest Rate (%)	12
Time In Loan — ○ Years ○ Months	4.28 Years or 51.34 Months
Monthly Payment ($)	300
Clear Calculate Close	

Figure 8.3: The program also incorporates a handy Loan Calculator that allows you to key in known or desired loan terms and has the program calculate missing terms for you. For example, if you want to borrow $12,000 for a new car at a 12% interest rate, how long will it take to pay off the loan if all you can afford is $300 per month? By keying in the known variables, the program provides you with an immediate answer: 51.34 months or 4.28 years. This handy feature allows you to do "what if" analysis on any loan term.

amortization table for the life of the loan, or for any loan year. Thus, you can find out exactly how much you will owe the bank at any specific future date should you wish to prepay the loan.

Although users with even moderate computer skills can create their own version of this program using their favorite spreadsheet, users without the expertise or time to create their own loan analysis spreadsheet will find this program very helpful in evaluating their financing options for a variety of loans.

Program Name: EZ Loan Manager 97® Version 4.20 © 1997
Program Type: Shareware (30 day evaluation)
Author's Name: Kevin Kai
E-Mail Address: gxc2@po.cwru.edu
Registration Fee: $10 (Payment should be sent to: Joy Chu, 145 Brittany Place, West Chester, PA 19380.)

General Evaluation: EZ Loan Manager 97 Version 4.20

	Excellent	Good	Average	Poor
Utility		***		
Ease of Use	***			
Ease of Learning	***			
Documentation			***	
Overall Rating		***		

The All-In-One Mortgage Calculator® Version 1.5

The All-In-One Mortgage Calculator (All-In-One) allows you to determine how much of a mortgage a typical bank is likely to approve given your current actual income and credit debt.

Using the program is simple: you input your actual monthly income and expenses into the first program screen, then click on the "Maximum Loan Amounts" tab and enter the interest and term of the loan. Based upon this information, the program tells you the maximum monthly payment for which you will likely qualify, and the highest priced home you will be able to purchase based on typical down payment ranging from 0-20%. You may also ask the program to figure the likely monthly payments including the mortgage and typical taxes on a home of any value for a fixed-term interest rate and duration of your choice.

All-In-One can be a useful tool in giving you a rough idea of the maximum mortgage and mortgage payment you can afford. Banks use somewhat different formulas in determining the debt to income ratio they will permit borrowers to bear; the actual ratio in any particular case can depend

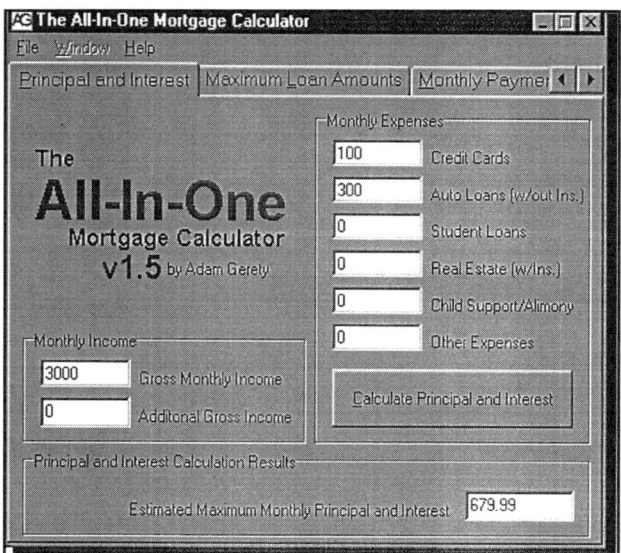

Figure 8.4: Input some basic information, and All-In-One will tell you the maximum monthly mortgage payment you can afford. In this example, a person who earns $3,000 gross income per month and has $400 in current monthly credit debt payments would qualify for a maximum mortgage of $679.99 per month.

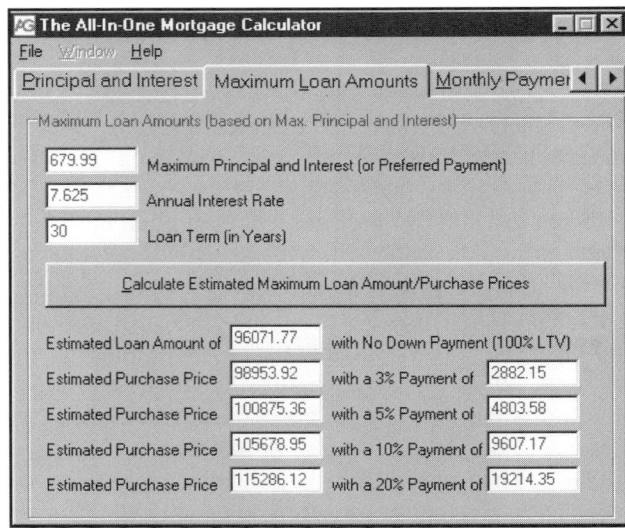

Figure 8.5: *Information from Principal and Interest screen is automatically carried over to the "Maximum Loan Amounts" screen, where the program shows the maximum purchase price for a home the borrower can afford.*

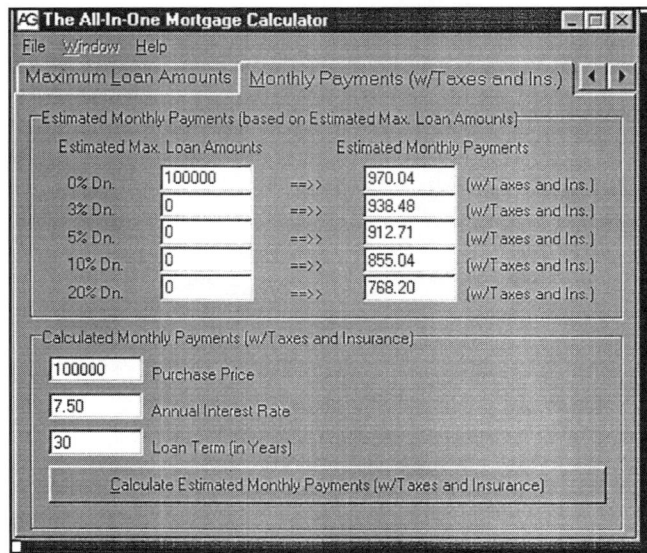

Figure 8.6: *All-In-One also allows borrowers to determine the approximate mortgage and real estate taxes payable monthly on a property of any given value financed at any interest rate and for any number of years.*

Chapter 8 : Loan Calculators

upon such factors as the borrower's credit worthiness, the size of the down payment, and the interest rate charged by the bank or other financial institution. Likewise, the actual real estate taxes a home buyer will need to pay will vary from state to state and within regions in a state. But the program's assumptions are reasonable averages that will at least give prospective buyers an idea of the maximum home price they can afford.

Program Name: The All-In-One Mortgage Calculator® Version 1.5
© 1996-1997
Program Type: Shareware
Author's Name: Adam Gerety
Address: 8634 Daytonia Avenue, Dallas, Texas 75218
Web Address: http://www.the-webguy.com/all-in-one
Registration Fee: $25

General Evaluation: The All-In-One Mortgage Calculator Version 6.3

	Excellent	Good	Average	Poor
Utility		***		
Ease of Use	***			
Ease of Learning	***			
Documentation			***	
Overall Rating			***	

CHAPTER 9

PRINTER TOOLS

One of the great advantages of Windows 95/98 is the ability it gives users to obtain excellent text and graphics output from even the most modest printers. Nonetheless, some printer management tasks remain a bit tedious, especially for novice users. Switching your default printer, or switching from a local to a network printer, for instance, can require navigating through several menus (e.g., Start-Settings-Control Panel through Windows, or File-Print-Select Printer in typical applications programs). Likewise, some simple tasks such as printing whatever is on your computer screen at any time are not as easily accomplished as in the good old DOS days, when the Print Screen key could be used to complete the task. In this chapter, we'll examine some representative programs available to extend and simplify the Windows 95/98 print function.

PrintKey® Version 2.0

PrintKey is a very handy small utility program that allows you to print either your entire desktop or any portion of it directly to the printer by pressing the Print Screen key.

This freeware program does not come with an installation utility. It must be decompressed from its ZIP file format and then manually run from Explorer. Alternatively, you can create a shortcut to the program or copy it to your StartUp folder so that it automatically loads on boot up (it requires only 250K bytes of RAM).

Once loaded, the program allows you to output the contents of your computer screen to your printer or to a bitmap file; you may then save on

Chapter 9 : Printer Tools

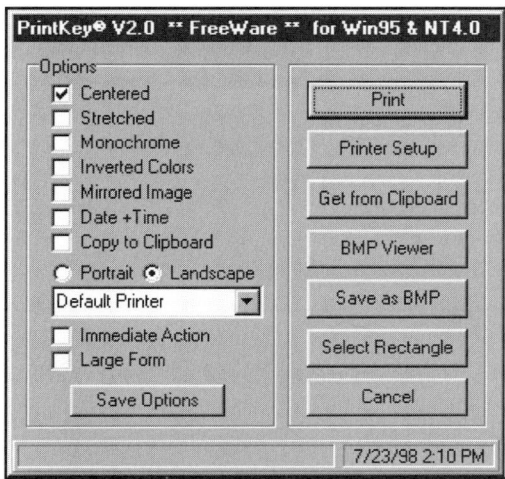

Figure 9.1: PrintKey Version 2.0 includes a simple user interface that makes the included documentation file almost superfluous.

disk. It can be configured to print automatically with options of your choosing or to present a dialogue box of options prior to printing (its default mode). Options include printer selection, centered, stretched, monochrome, inverted colors and mirrored image printing, printing the current date and time at the bottom of the printout, saving the captured screen to disk as a bitmap image, and printing in either landscape or portrait modes. You are also given the option to print only a portion of the screen by selecting it with the mouse. In addition, the program can be used to view bitmap images on disk and to load bitmap images from the Windows clipboard.

If you often need to print all or a portion of your computer screen, by all means give PrintKey a try. It will save you time, toner and paper, especially if you print out information from the Web on a regular basis, because it allows you select and print out only the information you need, rather than a multi-page HTML document. Best of all, its free. What more could you ask?

Program Name:	PrintKey® Version 2.0 © 1997
Program Type:	Freeware
Author's Name:	Alfred Bollinger
E-Mail Address:	coolmen@bluewin.ch
Web Address:	http://www.geocities.SiliconValley.com/Bay/3053
Registration Fee:	None

General Evaluation: PrintKey Version 2.0

	Excellent	Good	Average	Poor
Utility	***			
Ease of Use	***			
Ease of Learning	***			
Documentation			***	
Overall Rating	***			

Printscreen 95® Version 7.0

Printscreen 95 is another solid program that allows you to capture and print information on your screen via the Print Screen key. This program features both Windows and DOS screen capture/print capability, as well as the ability to print in color, monochrome or a fast two color (black and white) mode.

Figure 9.2: *Printscreen 95 Version 7.0 user interface*

This program features full install/uninstall capability, be run as a memory resident program (it can install itself on your StartUp directory as an option) and can also be accessed when needed from the Program folder or through Explorer. In addition to the ability to directly print screen images or save them as bitmap (BMP) files, the program permits you to print your entire screen, the active window or any portion of the screen you select with your mouse. It can also invert colors on the printout and stretch the screen contents to fill the entire printed page, thereby effectively magnifying the printed area (the aspect ratio on screens printed out with this option is not automatically maintained, however). In addition, you can elect to have the program print the current date, time and/or your name on every page.

Printscreen 95 is easy to set up, simple to use and includes excellent on-line help that most users will seldom need due to the program's intuitive interface.

Program Name:	Printscreen 95® Version 7.0 © 1997
Program Type:	Shareware (The program allows 50 uses before disabling itself.)
Company:	Super Simple Software
Address:	Glen Johnson, 2817 So. La Cienega Ave #B, Los Angeles, CA 90034
E-Mail Address:	glencj@sssware.com
Registration Fee:	$19.95 for one copy (Quantity discounts and site licenses are available.)

General Evaluation: Printscreen 95 Version 7.0

	Excellent	Good	Average	Poor
Utility	***			
Ease of Use	***			
Ease of Learning	***			
Documentation	***			
Overall Rating	***			

WPrinter Lite® Version 2.0

The multiple steps required to change or reconfigure your printer settings in Windows 95/98 can be a source of minor annoyance for the average user. Anyone who juggles a variety of local or network printers on a regular basis would find welcomed relief from WPrinter Lite, a simple program that allows you to change your printer or its configuration by clicking on an icon, rather than going through the normal Start-Settings-Printers sequence to gain access to change your printer setting or its setup configuration.

Once installed, the program places an icon in the System Tray area (the area on your desktop where the Windows clock and the icons for some programs that automatically load at startup reside). By pointing at the icon with your mouse, Windows will report the name of your current printer. Double-clicking on the icon brings up the familiar printer configuration dialog box that allows you to change your printer's normal settings (e.g., paper source, size, portrait or landscape orientation, number of copies to print and other printer-dependent commands and settings). Clicking on the right mouse button while pointing at the icon pops up a quick menu that allows you to change printers simply by selecting your choice from the installed printer list (See Figure 9.3). If you have both

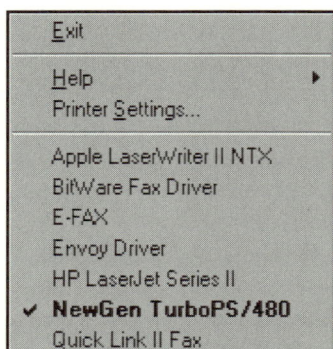

Figure 9.3: Right-clicking on WPrinter Lite's icon pops up a quick menu similar to this one, which shows my actual printer options. Individual printers and printer settings can easily and quickly be accessed from here, as can the program's help menu.

network and local printers installed on your system, these are represented by different icons. In addition, the printer settings and a help menu can also be accessed through this quick menu.

Even if you do not use more than a single printer in your system, WPrinter can still be a valuable asset, allowing you to configure your printer under various options and save these as printer drivers with different names. For example, if you have a high-resolution laser printer, you can configure four drivers with the following settings: Driver1: 800 dpi resolution; Driver2: 400 dpi resolution; Driver3: 150 dpi resolution; Driver4: 400 dpi resolution with two copies. In this way, you can easily change the resolution of your printer to match your needs, not wasting toner (and time) on high resolution draft output, or you can choose a driver to automatically print duplicate copies on demand (driver 4 in the above example).

For users who need more flexibility than featured in the Lite version of this program, a commercial version (WPrinter Pro 2.0) is available for $18.95 for a single copy, with substantial discounts for two or more copies. The professional version of the program includes many more features with greater printer control options including print orientation, number of copies, add a printer wizard, and print cue control among others. It is also available as shareware with a 30-day evaluation period.

Program Name:	WPrinter Lite® Version 2.0 © 1996-1997
Program Type:	Freeware (WPrinter Version 2.0 Pro is available as shareware with a 30- day evaluation period.)
Company:	USysWare
Address:	NorthStar Solutions, PO Box 25262, Columbia, SC 29224
E-Mail Address:	smish@mindspring.com

Registration Fee: None (WPrinter Pro Version 2.0 is available at a cost of $18.95 for a single copy, less in quantities of two or more.)

General Evaluation: WPrinter Lite Version 2.0

	Excellent	Good	Average	Poor
Utility		***		
Ease of Use	***			
Ease of Learning	***			
Documentation		***		
Overall Rating		***		

CHAPTER 10
TIME TOOLS

In this chapter we'll examine a potpourri of helpful and interesting programs relating to time and timekeeping that should bring a twinkle to the most hardened clock watcher's eye.

RoundClock® Version 2.0

RoundClock 2.0 is a neat clock program with a number of features beyond displaying the current time. Once loaded, the program lives up to its name by displaying a movable round clock on your current open window or desktop (Double clicking on the clock changes it to a square clock face and allows you to change its size.) Given that Windows 95/98 already displays the current time in the System Tray, this feature of itself is of little value, except perhaps for obsessive clock watchers who simply must have a clock in the margin as they work. But this is not RoundClock's only feature. The program also offers multiple alarm functions that can play customizable sounds and display reminder messages on screen. Perhaps most useful of all is RoundClock's ability to launch any program at a preset time, allowing you to customize routine applications such as backing up your data or performing a disk scan at predetermined convenient times during the day, such as during your lunch hour or while you sleep. Applications that need user input to start can be automatically launched and will await the user's response. (Even if your particular tape backup program cannot launch and run unattended, it is would surely receive your immediate attention if it opens automatically at its appointed time while you're working on another application.)

Chapter 10 : Time Tools

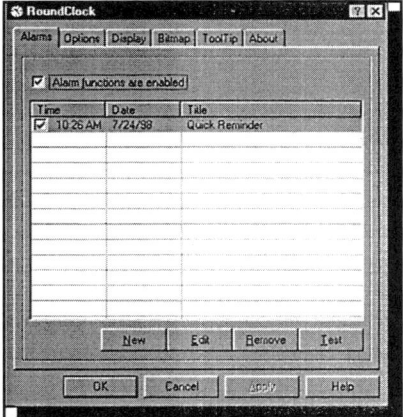 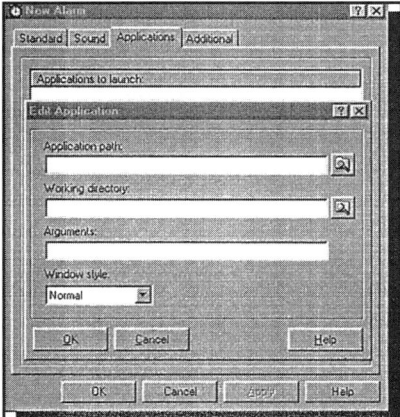

Figure 10.1 (left): RoundClock offers a surprising array of customizable features that include multiple reminder memos and alarms that can display messages on screen and play predefined sounds or the WAV file of your choice. *Figure 10.2 (right):* A useful feature of RoundClock is its ability to launch multiple programs automatically at preset times.

Aside from the curiosity value of being able to display a different type of clock than the Windows default within your applications, this program's alarm and reminder functions together with its ability to preschedule the launch of multiple programs make RoundClock a useful tool.

Program Name:	RoundClock® Version 2.0 © 1997
Program Type:	Shareware (30-day evaluation period.)
Company:	fkWare (Frank Kintrup)
Address:	Frank Kintrup, Foelsener Weg 21, D-33100 Paderborn, Germany
E-Mail Address:	sales@fkware.com
Registration Fee:	$10 for a single copy, less in quantities of two or more.

General Evaluation: RoundClock Version 2.0

	Excellent	Good	Average	Poor
Utility		***		
Ease of Use	***			
Ease of Learning	***			
Documentation	***			
Overall Rating		***		

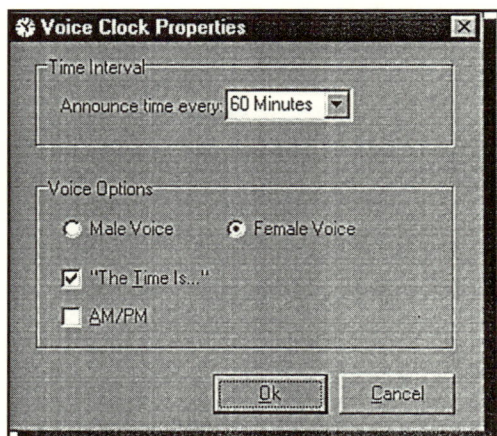

Figure 10.3: *Available options in Voice Clock include a male or female voice and the frequency of the time announcements. For those users who may have difficulty discerning night from day, the program can also announce whether the time is AM or PM.*

Voice Clock® Version 1.2

Voice Clock is a simple program that tells the time with either a male or female voice on hourly, half-hourly or quarter-hourly user selected intervals using your system's sound card.

After the program is decompressed, it can be run from Explorer or added to your Start-Up folder for automatic loading upon bootup. Once loaded, the program resides on your System Tray and can be disabled by right-clicking on its clock icon. The program's Properties and Help menus are also available by right-clicking on the System Tray icon.

Program Name:	Voice Clock® Version 1.2 © 1997
Program Type:	Shareware (30- day evaluation period.)
Programmer:	Scott Lanford
Address:	5416 Nations Ford Rd., Charlotte, NC 28217
Registration Fee:	$5

General Evaluation: Voice Clock Version 1.2

	Excellent	*Good*	*Average*	*Poor*
Utility		***		
Ease of Use	***			
Ease of Learning	***			
Documentation	***			
Overall Rating		***		

TimeRC® Version 2.0

Setting your system clock quickly and accurately has never been simpler, thanks to TimeRC, a terrific freeware program that allows you to synchronize you system clock with that of the U.S. Naval Observatory or 30 other highly reliable servers over the Internet.

In order to run TimeRC you must be connected to the Internet via a network or dial-up connection. When the program is run, it logs on to the site of your choice (U.S. Naval Observatory, by default) and automatically updates your system clock to the nearest second. It automatically adjusts the time to your time zone and to standard/daylight savings time by extracting that information from your Windows 95/98 settings.

In addition to the ability to accurately update your system's clock, the program provides a range of additional thoughtful features that most users will appreciate. These include information as to the sun's distance from the earth (a mere 151,959,600 miles at the time of this writing), the start and end dates for daylight savings time, detailed moon phase information (see Figure 10.5) and even detailed information on upcoming meteor showers.

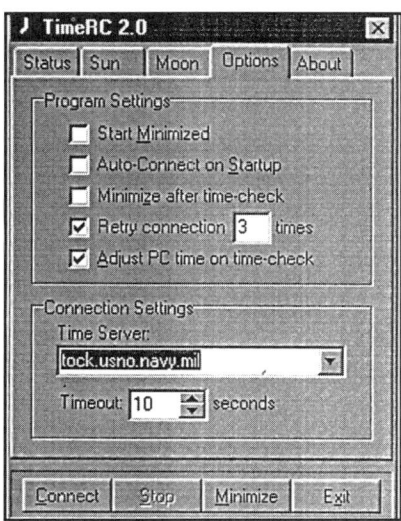 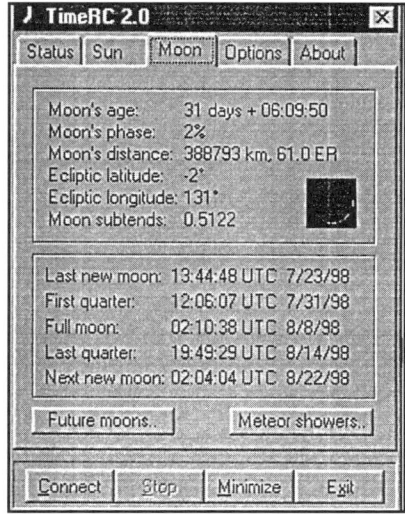

Figure 10.4 (left): TimeRC allows you to synchronize your system clock with the U.S. Naval Observatory's nuclear clock or choice of 30 other reliable sites. *Figure 10.5 (right):* Information about the sun, moon and meteor showers is also available as an added bonus. The moon's current 2% phase is barely detectable as a white sliver in the lower right hand corner of its graphic representation above.

TimeRC is a wonderful little program that you should download and try. To its author's credit, it boasts the additional benefit of being absolutely free.

Program Name:	TimeRC® Version 2.0 © 1997
Program Type:	Freeware
Programmer:	Karl Sudar
E-Mail Address:	kfsudar@mailbox.syr.edu
Registration Fee:	None.

General Evaluation: Voice Clock Version 1.2

	Excellent	Good	Average	Poor
Utility	***			
Ease of Use	***			
Ease of Learning	***			
Documentation	***			
Overall Rating	***			

Time95® Version 1.20

Time95 is a simple world clock program with the ability to simultaneously show the time in five cities from its database of 250 cities.

Once you decompress the program's ZIP file into the directory of your choice, you can run Time95 directly through Explorer by copying a shortcut to the program's executable file (Time95.exe), or by copying the file to your Start-Up directory. Once loaded, you will need to input some environment settings that include your location and daylight or standard time setting, whether you wish a 12 or 24 hour clock, and whether you desire the program to run minimized or always on top of your current application. You can then choose up to five cities, one from each of the following three classifications: North American Cities, Asian Cities, and Australia and Pacific Cities, and two from the classification of European Cities. This shareware release is decidedly Euro-centric and ignores some notable world regions. Fortunately, by the time you read this, a new version of the program should be available in shareware form; it promises to allow for user-selected cities and states, as well as incorporate a clickable world map (click on the country of your choice and get its current time).

Even with its limitations, however, this program can be very helpful if you make overseas calls on a regular basis to any cities the program supports.

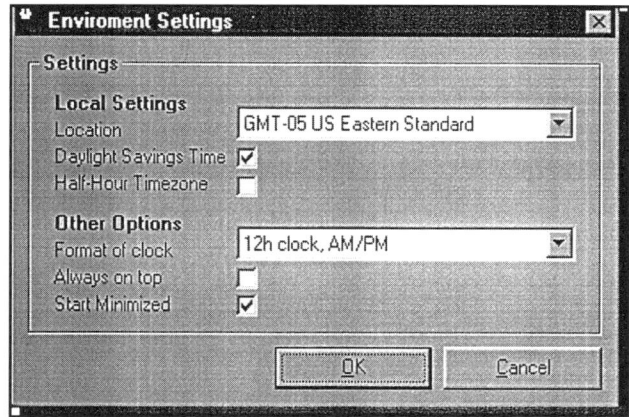

Figure 10.6: Although you must manually set system variables prior to using the program, Time95 makes the process fast and easy.

Figure 10.7: You may choose five cities from a database of 250. Though all regions of the world are not represented by this version of the program, expanded coverage is promised in its next major release.

Program Name:	Time95® Version 1.20 © 1995-1997
Program Type:	Shareware (30-day evaluation period.)
Programmer:	Henrik Holdt
E-Mail Address:	henrikh@kagi.com
Web Page:	http://www.kagi.com/henrikh
Address:	Kagi, 1442-A Walnut Street #392-B3, Berkeley, California, 94709-1405
Registration Fee:	$10 (Quantity discounts available if purchasing more than 4 licenses.)

General Evaluation: Time95 Version 1.20

	Excellent	Good	Average	Poor
Utility		***		
Ease of Use	***			
Ease of Learning	***			
Documentation		***		
Overall Rating		***		

CHAPTER 11
PERSONAL INFORMATION MANAGEMENT

Do you find yourself having difficulty with organizing your workday, scheduling appointments and keeping track of important projects? For the average professional with limited secretarial support, the answer is likely to be "yes" to all of the above. Many users have found that having a PC or network terminal on their desk can actually hinder productivity; keeping track of the flood of information from e-mail to information downloaded from the Web can sometimes seem a full time job (not to mention the extraordinarily effective ways that the PC provides to waste time, such as playing solitaire games and on-line shopping, to name but two). But take heart; help is available from your computer in the guise of personal information management programs that can help you regain control of your workday, improve your productivity, and prevent your computer from becoming a virtual black hole on your desk capable of absorbing your energy, time, and creativity, leaving behind a bleary eyed void.

Executive Desk '97®

Executive Desk '97 is a well implemented, easy to use personal information manager with a variety of powerful features.

The program incorporates a full-featured address book that allows you to keep track of all personal and business contacts. Unlike many address book programs that limit you to name, address and telephone fields, this program, provides great flexibility in the type of data fields that

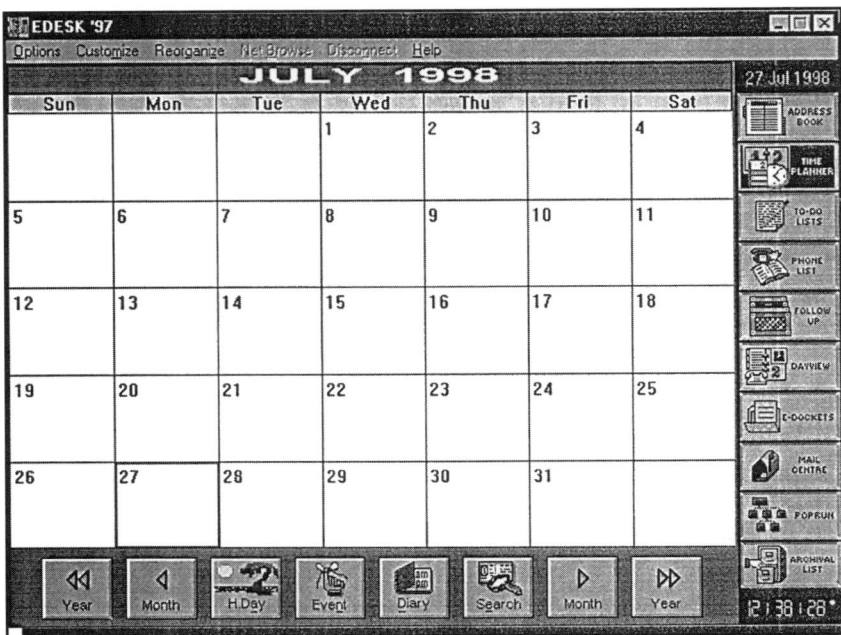

Figure 11.1: Executive Desk '97 permits you to plan your business and personal schedule years into the future, giving you great flexibility to track projects and update, prioritize and change entries as the need arises.

it accepts, including e-mail, fax and cellular phone numbers, and even the preferred salutation for each contact. Free-form notes can also be incorporated into each contact's entry, and the program can dial the home, business or cell phone number for you while the information remains on the screen for your easy reference and note taking.

The program's planner module allows you to plan your schedule years ahead, and browse any past or future scheduled data at will. Daily entries allow you to schedule meetings and then easily annotate and update information about the scheduled event. Follow-up information may also be used (e.g., the need to follow up in the future with a letter or phone call, and the status of such follow-up at the current time.). Files can be easily attached to each entry, so that the minutes from a business meeting, for example, can be attached to the calendar entry for the meeting—an excellent feature not found in many similar programs.

Executive Desk '97 also incorporates a flexible "to-do" list. Items on the list can be assigned a low, medium or high priority and the status of each item can be tracked and updated until it is completed. (Status options

Chapter 11 : Personal Information Management

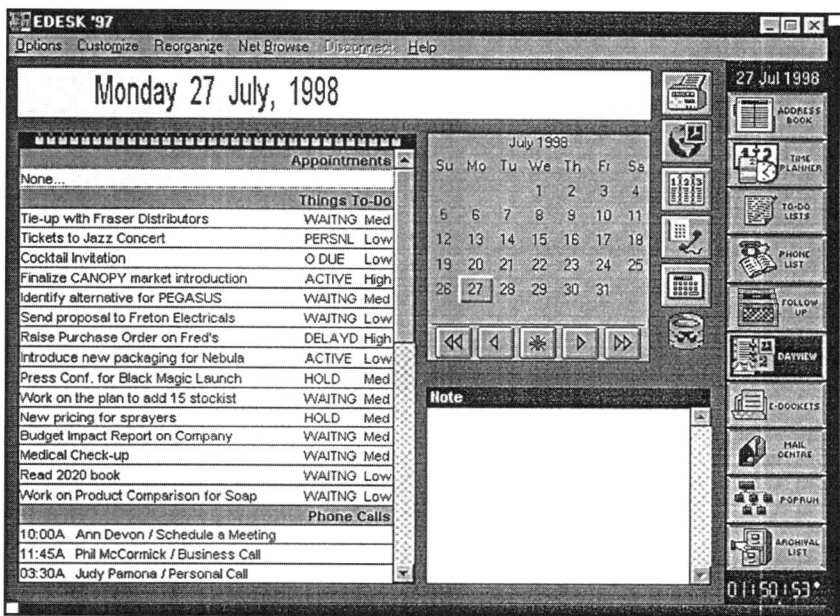

Figure 11.2: Viewing your daily schedule and tracking your progress on pending tasks is a simple, quick process. In addition, telephone logs, detailed follow-up information and the status of pending tasks are all a few mouseclicks away. The program can even integrate with your Web browser, e-mail program and Timex Data Link watch for greater flexibility.

include new, waiting, delayed, on-time, overdue, VIP, normal and urgent.) Notes or file attachments can be added or updated for each project as needed. All pending projects can be sorted and displayed by due date, status or priority.

The program also includes a phone contact manager that allows information on all personal and business calls to be tracked, annotated and saved for future reference. This feature can be especially useful to consultants and other professionals who bill clients for their logged telephone time. The purpose of the call can be catalogued, information about the call annotated and the time and duration of the call logged.

Executive Desk '97 incorporates a number of additional features that include the ability to integrate with your e-mail and Web browser. For example, a wonderful world time clock utility is available for use with the program. It pops up the four world cities of your choice and gives you the current time in each of these cities—a useful feature when making overseas calls to clients or associates. A program launcher is also included that allows you to launch your favorite programs directly from Executive Desk '97. You can even uplink and download data with your Timex Data Link watch, if you own one. Of course, full database search, sort and print options are available.

In all, this is an extremely well integrated, useful program that, for all its flexibility and features, is remarkably easy to learn and use.

Program Name:	Executive Desk '97® © 1994-1997
Program Type:	Shareware (60-day evaluation period.)
Company:	SOFTPLUS International
Address:	PsL, P.O. Box 35705, Houston, TX 77235-5705
E-Mail Address:	softplus@compuserve.com
Web Page:	http:/www.linax.ch/edesk
Registration Fee:	$49.95

General Evaluation: Executive Desk '97

	Excellent	Good	Average	Poor
Utility	***			
Ease of Use	***			
Ease of Learning	***			
Documentation	***			
Overall Rating	***			

Time & Chaos 32® Version 5.3.2

Time & Chaos 32 is another good personal information management program with many customizable features.

The program includes a calendar, appointment manager, dialer and to-do list, all of which can be viewed on a single screen, or you can zoom in on any individual module of the program via a quick menu available when you click the right mouse button. When viewing the calendar in zoom mode, you can view a month at a time (with partial appointment notations visible), or double-click on a specific date to view a week's worth of appointments at once.

The program's telephone book allows you to enter not just the traditional name and address information of a simple index-card type database program, but highly customizable information that includes name, up to two full addresses per entry (e.g., home and business), business and home telephones, fax, e-mail, and pager numbers, and up to 12 additional

Chapter 11 : Personal Information Management

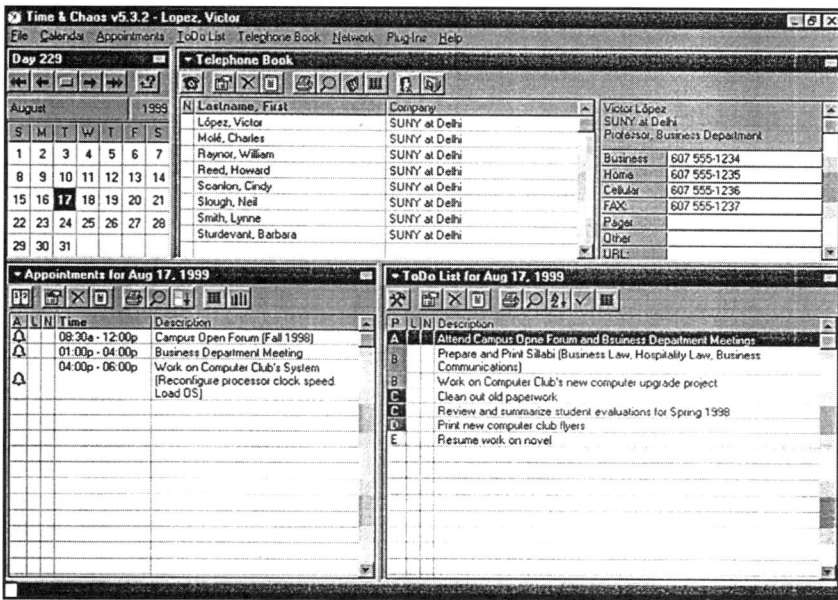

Figure 11.3: Time & Chaos 32 provides a clean, no-nonsense interface that allows all information to be viewed in a single screen. For a closer look, you can zoom to any of the program's windows via a quick menu accessible through the right mouse button.

customized fields of your choice for the creation of a true custom contacts database. Extensive information may also be linked to each entry by attaching one or more text or graphics files; extensive memos may also be written with the built-in text editor and attached to any entry. Records from the telephone book can be linked to schedules meetings or to-do lists; this feature is very useful in linking people with the activities in which they participate, thus making it easier to, for example, follow up on events or ongoing projects with people who participated in them.

You can use the data in the telephone book to automatically dial your phone or send faxes or e-mails with a MAPI mail program like Microsoft Exchange. The program can also integrate with your favorite Web browser and be set up to allow for e-mail communication within an Intranet network. Naturally, the data in the telephone book can be sorted, searched and output to a printer.

While Time & Chaos 32 may lack some of the glitzy graphics and power buttons of some other commercial and shareware PIMs, the program provides a simple, usable interface that works quickly and well. In

Unit II : Personal Productivity

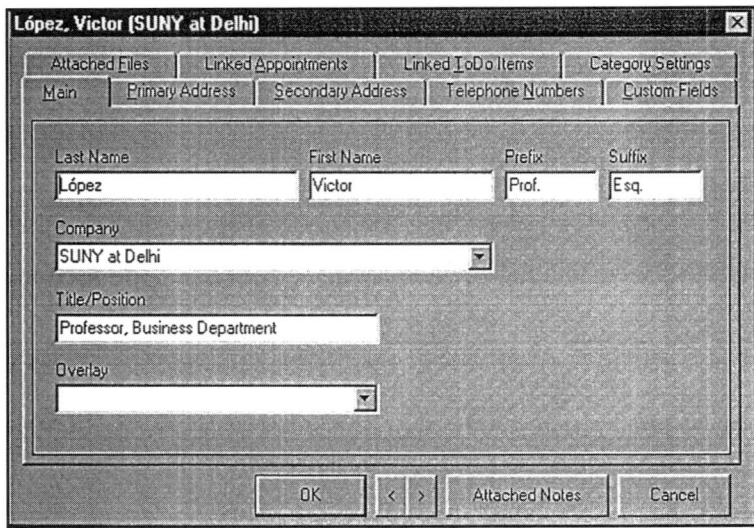

Figure 11.4: Up to 12 custom fields may be created for any telephone book entry, along with a primary and secondary address. Add to this the ability to link multiple external files and memos to each record, as well as the capacity to link telephone book records to calendar appointments and to-do lists, and you can begin to appreciate the program's great flexibility.

addition, it provides some highly customizable features that allow it to approximate a true database program rather than a mere phone book dialer.

Program Name:	Time & Chaos 32® Version 5.3.2 © 1992–1997
Program Type:	Shareware (21-day evaluation period)
Company:	iSBiSTER International, Inc.
Address:	1111 Beltline Rd., Suite 204, Garland, TX 75040
E-Mail Address:	sales@isbister.com
Web Page:	http:/www.isbister.com
Registration Fee:	$45

General Evaluation: Time & Chaos 32 Version 5.3.2

	Excellent	*Good*	*Average*	*Poor*
Utility	***			
Ease of Use	***			
Ease of Learning	***			
Documentation	***			
Overall Rating	***			

UNIT III
EDUCATIONAL PROGRAMS

The personal computer's usefulness as a teaching and training tool has been exploited from the earliest days of personal computing. Educational software has been among the first type of applications software developed not only for the current IBM and Apple platforms, but for their early precursors as well, including the Commodore, Texas Instruments, Atari and similar early computer makers. The tradition continues today with a wide variety of commercial as well as shareware and freeware offerings such as the representative samples of testing, speed reading, courseware and grading programs you will find in the next four chapters.

Test Construction Set supports a variety of exam question types, including true false, multiple choice, and fill-the-blank questions. (One, two or three blanks in selected order or random order form are supported for fill-in questions.) In addition, the program allows for "hotspot" answer selection, a method by which the test taker is asked to click on a graphic image or menu choice on-screen to select the correct answer to a question.

A variety of security tools are available to the test creator to ensure the exam's integrity. These include the ability to assign passwords to individual exam takers as well as the option to limit the number of times an exam can be accessed. The program also allows for restricting access to any other Windows program while an exam is in progress; if this option is selected, the program disallows access to any other program until an exam is completed and its results saved. In addition, the time a user may

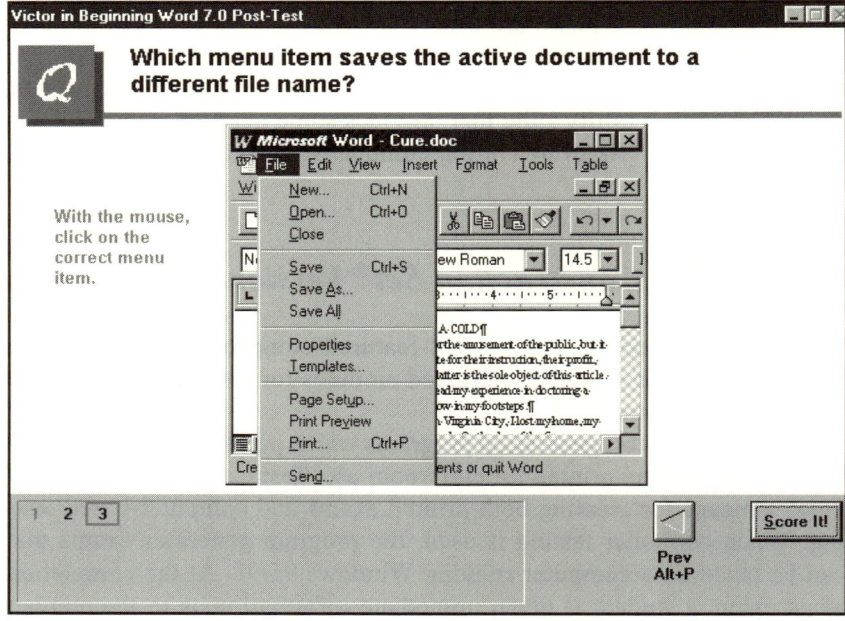

Figure 12.1: Among Test Construction System's most useful feature is the ability to create computerized tests that allow a user to click on the correct answers to questions right on the screen. After clicking on the correct answer, a user can click on the "Score It" button and get immediate feedback on whether the question was answered correctly. The program can be set up to give auditory and visual messages to accompany each correct or incorrect answer, such as applause when an answer is correct followed by various levels of praise.

have to take a given exam can also be restricted by the test creator if timed exams are desired.

Although an on-line manual is not available, the help files and sample tests that accompany the trial version of Test Construction Set make exam preparation and exam production fairly uncomplicated for users with basic computer literacy skills. The test creation process is slower than in many of the testing programs I've used in the past, but the highly professional-looking exams that this program generates are worth the extra effort and time it takes to prepare them—especially in a context where a single exam may be used many times or where the integration of graphics is essential to the testing process. The program shines in particular when the "hotspot" test option is used to require a user to select a graphic image or click on the appropriate area of the screen to select the correct answer. As you can see in Figure 12.1, this option can be very useful when testing such areas as program-specific competencies. Asking a student to click on the appropriate icon or menu option in answer to a specific question is a much more realistic and natural means of assessing the student's familiarity with a software package than attempting to assess the same knowledge through a true false or multiple choice question.

Program Name:	Test Construction Set® Version 3.0.7 © 1994
Program Type:	Demo
Company Name:	Computer Training & Support Corporation
Web Page:	http://www.ctsc.com/tcs.htm
E-mail:	sales@ctsc.com
Registration Fee:	Contact sales@ctsc.com for current pricing.

General Evaluation: Test Construction Set Version 3.0.7

	Excellent	*Good*	*Average*	*Poor*
Utility		***		
Ease of Use		***		
Ease of Learning		***		
Documentation				***
Overall Rating		***		

True Test® Version 1.20

True Test is a test creation package that allows a user to generate multiple choice tests and to administer tests to students either in a class or lab setting by distributing copies via floppy disk.

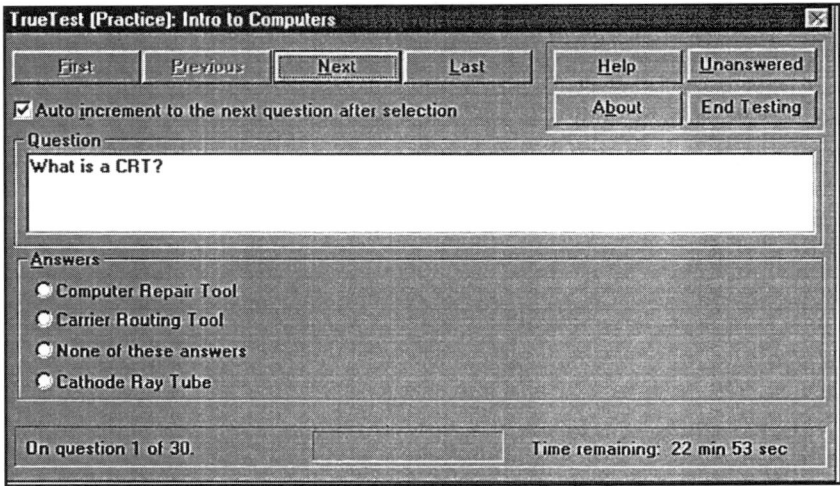

Figure 12.2: *True Test offers a simple, no-frills solution for the creation and administration of computer-based multiple choice tests. Questions advance automatically once a test taker clicks on one of the available answers, and a running timer at the lower right of the screen reminds the test taker of the remaining time for completing the exam. Once the floppy disk containing the test and the test taker's answers is returned to the instructor or proctor, an answer sheet can easily be generated with a numerical grade that can be printed and returned to the student.*

Although the program is limited to multiple choice testing, it provides sufficient flexibility so as to make it a useful tool for skills assessment or for purposes of administering practice tests. It provides adequate security features such as password protection and an automatic test locking feature that gives the test giver the option to prevent access to a test once it has been taken, thereby effectively preventing a user from taking the same test twice. It also offers randomized question order and answer order on multiple versions of the same test, making it difficult for students to copy from one another during test sessions.

True Test comes complete with several sample tests and brief but very useful documentation. The program's help files provide a brief tutorial with step-by-step instructions for creating a sample test. While not the most powerful test creation package available, True Test provides a simple solution for faculty who wish to create computer-based multiple choice exams that can be administered within and outside of the classroom in a simple, secure and effective manner.

Program Name:	True Test® Version 1.20 © 1997
Program Type:	Shareware (30 day evaluation)
Company Name:	MaeDae Enterprises
Company Address:	5805 Prospero Road
	Peyton, CO 80831
Web Page:	http://www.maedae.com
Registration Fee:	Contact info@maedae.com for current pricing.

General Evaluation: True Test Version 1.20

	Excellent	*Good*	*Average*	*Poor*
Utility		***		
Ease of Use		***		
Ease of Learning		***		
Documentation		***		
Overall Rating		***		

Training Tools® Version 3.0

As its name implies, Training Tools is a small utility suite of programs that are intended to facilitate computer instruction and group presentations that utilize a video projection system.

Multimedia presentations have become increasingly popular in business and academe in recent years. Anyone who uses a computer display projection system and presentation software to assist in the delivery of sales presentations, employee training, classroom education or any other purpose will appreciate the three simple but useful tools offered in this package: Mag Lense, PC Chalkboard and Quick Sound. Each of the utilities can be installed in the system tray and called up by clicking on their respective icons.

The first utility, Mag Lense, pops up a virtual magnifying glass in the upper left hand corner of your display that magnifies any area of your screen over which you scroll your mouse, as Figure 12.3 illustrates. You can position the magnifying glass anywhere on the desktop by clicking and dragging it like a normal graphics image; you can also resize it in much the same way. The significant magnification it offers to any area over which the mouse pointer is dragged can make it easier to see power buttons, icons and small graphic details in programs that are sometimes too small to view clearly—especially by viewers who may be sitting towards the back of the room.

96 Unit III : Educational Programs

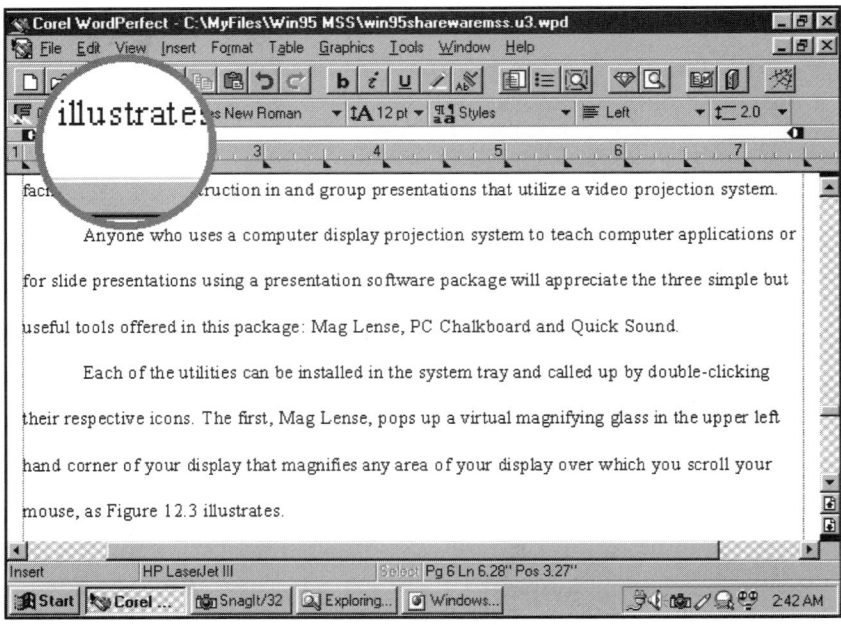

Figure 12.3: Mag Lense

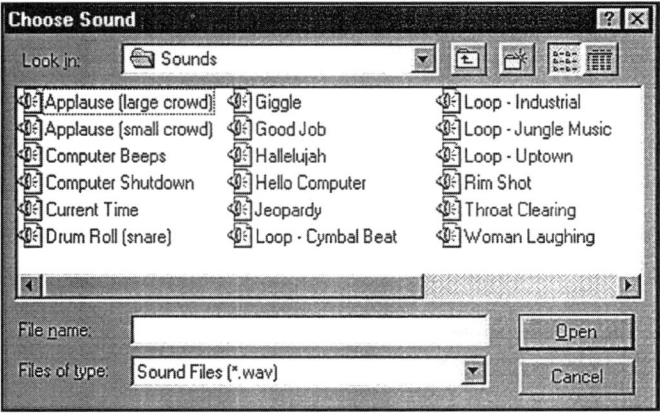

Figure 12.4: Quick Sound

The second program, PC Chalkboard, turns the normal mouse pointer into a virtual whiteboard marker that allows the user to underline or circle and area of the screen or highlight portions of the screen by holding down the left mouse button while moving the marker pointer over the area to be selected. After marking the screen, double clicking of the PC Chalkboard icon automatically erases the markings and returns the pointer to the normal pointer.

Finally, Quick Sound allows for the quick insertion of a variety of sounds at any time within a presentation to help liven it up (or to awaken sleepy viewers?). The available WAV files are listed in Figure 12.4, but these can easily be expanded by copying the WAV files of your choice to the appropriate directory. A hot key can also be selected as an alternative to double-clicking on the program's icon in the system tray.

Program Name: Training Tools® Version 3.0 © 1997
Program Type: Shareware
Company Name: Milori Software
Company Address: P.O. Box 52182
Raleigh, NC 27612
Web Page: http://www.milori.com
Registration Fee: $39.95

General Evaluation: Training Tools Version 3.0

	Excellent	Good	Average	Poor
Utility	***			
Ease of Use	***			
Ease of Learning	***			
Documentation			***	
Overall Rating	***			

CHAPTER 13
SPEED READING

Personal computers and the information explosion associated with the World Wide Web have made it more important than ever for the average person to improve his or her reading speed and comprehension. Fortunately, a number or varied tools and approaches exist for improving reading speed, from traditional classroom-based speed reading courses to books, tapes and now your personal computer. In this chapter, we will examine a single terrific program that can help you to read faster without sacrificing reading comprehension.

AceReader® Version 3.2

AceReader is a dual-purpose powerful personal productivity training tool that can significantly improve your reading speed. The program incorporates two distinct training modes. The first, termed *Rapid Serial Visual Presentation* (RSVP), flashes words on the center of the computer screen in one to five word segments (selected by the user). The advantage of this technique is that it permits information to be absorbed faster than in traditional left-to-right scanning mode; the eyes need not move since text is flashed at the center of the screen. While this form of "reading" can seem a bit awkward at first, it can potentially enhance concentration and reduce eye strain. After only a few minutes with the program, I found RSVP a quite natural way to read that minimizes the normal peripheral distractions incidental to the normal reading process. The second training mode, *Tachistoscopic Scroll Presentation,* flashes words on the screen from left to right in one to five word chunks of text, at the user's option.

Chapter 13 : Speed Reading

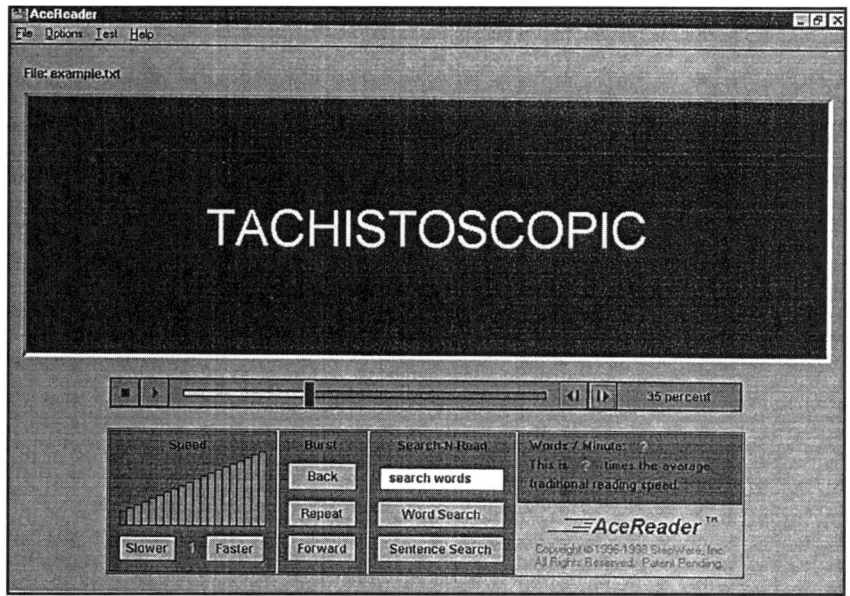

Figure 13.1: AceReader running in RSVP mode. The length of the string of text that displays in the center screen area of the program can be preset by the user from one to five words. The speed with which words appear, the delay between text strings and even the font face and font size can all be selected by the user to meet his or her individual preferences.

This method of presentation closely mirrors the natural way we are all trained to read in Western languages.

For users who wish to improve their reading speed of traditional printed materials, the *Tachistoscopic Scroll Presentation* method is probably preferable as a means of improving reading speed and reading comprehension. The *Rapid Serial Visual Presentation*, or RSVP, training method will be appealing primarily to users who wish to filter electronic text through the AceReader program to utilize RSVP reading. The program makes this possible by permitting users to filter any text copied to the Windows clipboard through AceReader for an RSVP presentation. With sustained practice using this method, you can retrain yourself to read any printed material one or more lines at once by scanning down the center of a printed page.

AceReader's high degree of adaptability makes it an extremely useful tool for nearly any reader, regardless of current reading level or reading speed. Highly recommended.

Unit III : Educational Programs

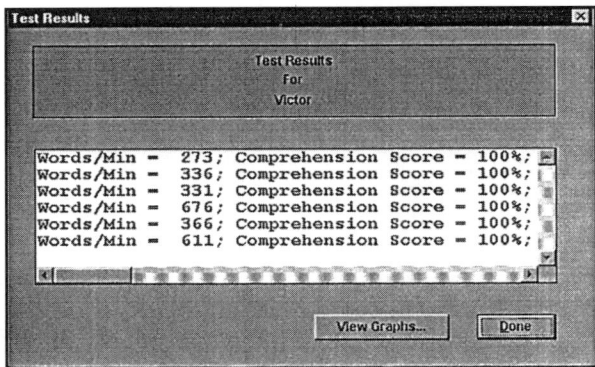

Figure 13.2: The shareware demo version of this program allows users to test their reading speed and reading comprehension in a series of seven different tests and even outputs the data as a graph for tracking purposes. The registered version of this program contains 72 different tests.

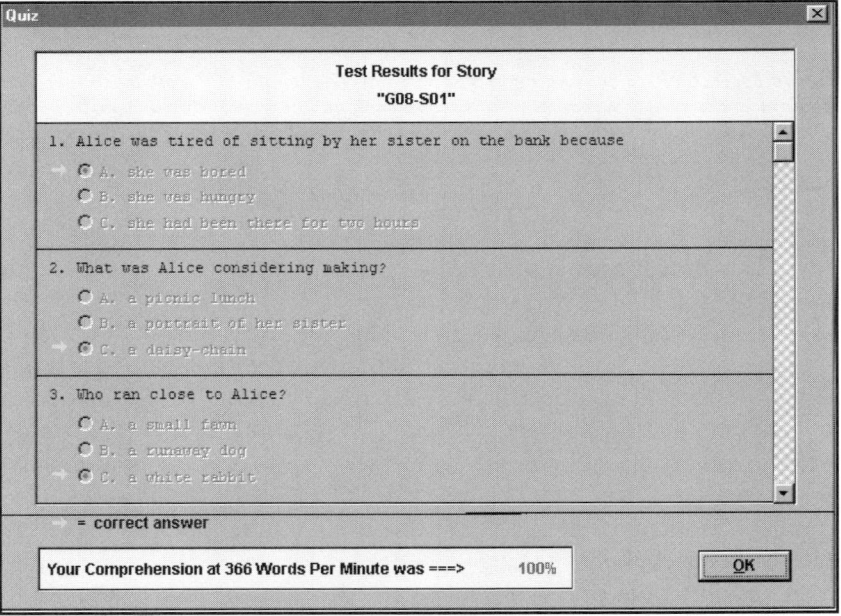

Figure 13.3: After taking a test, reading speed and comprehension are reported and kept on file for each user. The highest permitted testing speed for the RSVP mode is level 11 or 20 available speed levels, or just over 366 words per minute (better than 1.5 times the average reading speed). The registered version will permit substantially higher testing speeds by users up to the 20 available speed levels.

Program Name:	AceReader® Version 3.2 © 1996-98 (Patent Pending)
Program Type:	Shareware Demo (30 day evaluation)
Company Name:	StepWare, Inc.
Company Address:	1750 30th Street Suite 632 Boulder, CO USA 80301
E-mail:	sales@setsystems.com
Registration Fee:	$24.95 (Quantity and educational discounts available.)

General Evaluation: AceReader Version 3.2

	Excellent	*Good*	*Average*	*Poor*
Utility	***			
Ease of Use	***			
Ease of Learning	***			
Documentation	***			
Overall Rating	***			

CHAPTER 14
COURSEWARE

Learning a new software package can be a frustrating experience for the average user. While users' manuals have undeniably become more user-friendly and, in many cases, are actually quite useful these days, the average computer user still requires more hand-holding and instruction than these typically provide. Fortunately, unlike the luckless computer user pioneers of the late 1970's and early 1980's who were left largely to their own devices in learning obtuse, intimidating software for their DOS-based computers, today's computer users have a wealth of resources in learning new programs. Aftermarket instructional and reference books are available for the leading software packages, as are computer-based tutorials, training videos and both credit and non-credit college class offerings. To this list, users can now add free, computer-based courseware thanks to ChalkSoft's Courseware Web series, a sampling of whose excellent computer-related courses are reviewed next.

ChalkSoft's Courseware Web® Series

ChalkSoft's Courseware Web series is not technically Windows 95/98 software, but rather a series of well constructed course lessons using HTML documents viewable with any standard Web browser, such as Microsoft's Internet Explorer or Netscape's Communicator. Because they are not stand-alone Windows 95/98 software packages, these courseware offerings must be installed a bit differently than traditional software. Fortunately, the courses are distributed in self-extracting archive files that make the installation process simple. After downloading a specific course

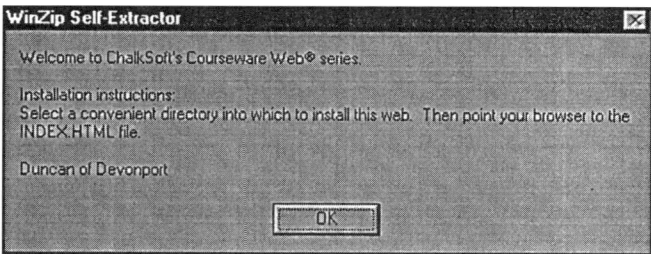

Figure 14.1: By running the self-extracting archive file containing each course, you will be prompted with the only instructions you need to install and run the HTML files that make up each course.

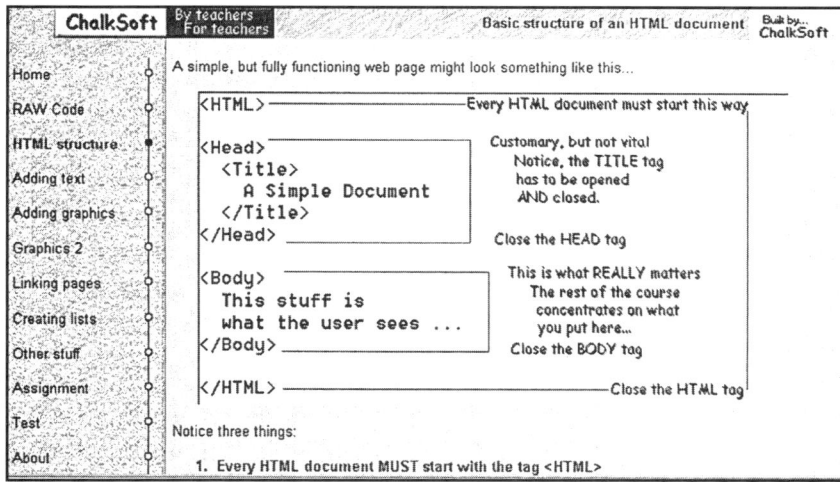

Figure 14.2: Partial screen captured from ChalkSoft's HTML Programming Courseware Web Series.

from ChalkSoft's web page, you simply double-click on the course file using Windows Explorer; as the self-extracting archive loads, it prompts you to select the directory and drive to which you wish to install the necessary files, and asks you to load the file **Index.htm** with your Web browser. (See Figure 14.1) You can load the file and launch the HTML course simply by double-clicking on the **Index.htm** file within Windows Explorer.

As Figures 14.2–14.4 show, each course is a self-contained complete lesson that users can complete at their own pace. The samples shown here are from three of the currently available courses dealing with HTML programming, Microsoft Word 7.0 and Microsoft Power Point. For a complete

Unit III : Educational Programs

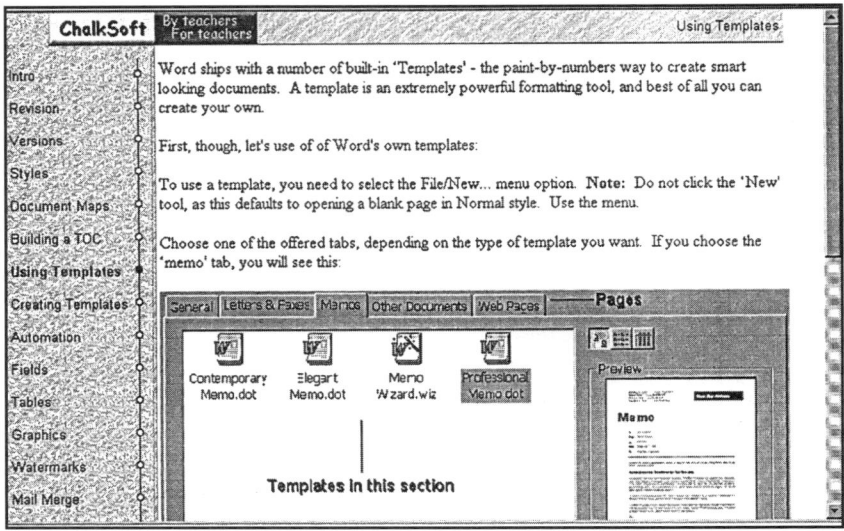

Figure 14.3: Partial screen capture from ChalkSoft's Microsoft Word 7 Courseware Web Series.

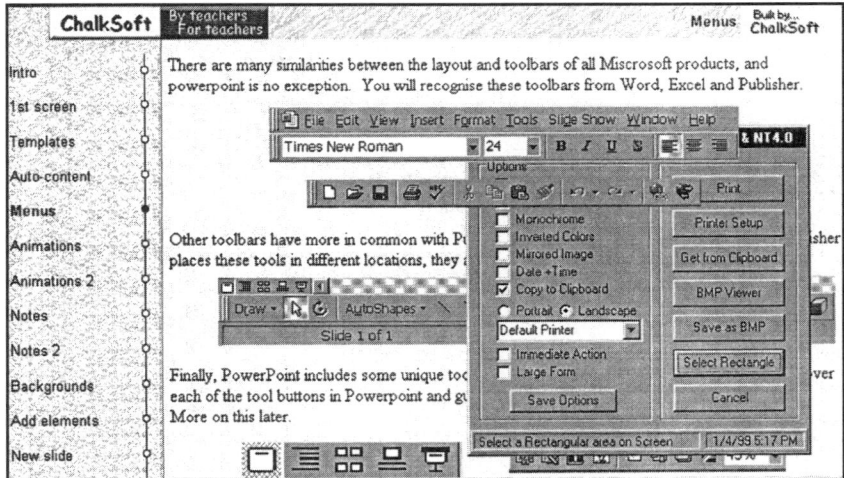

Figure 14.4: Partial screen capture from ChalkSoft's Microsoft PowerPoint Courseware Web Series.

Chapter 14 : Courseware

current list of course offerings and educational shareware programs available for evaluation, visit ChalkSoft at its home page, **www.chalksoft.com.** You can also contact the company via e-mail at **info@chalksoft.com** for more information.

Program Name:	ChalkSoft's Courseware Web® Series ©1998
Program Type:	Freeware
Company Name:	ChalkSoft
Web Page:	http://www.chalksoft.com
E-Mail:	info@chalksoft.com
Registration Fee:	None

General Evaluation: ChalkSoft Courseware Web Series

	Excellent	*Good*	*Average*	*Poor*
Utility	***			
Ease of Use	***			
Ease of Learning	***			
Documentation				***
Overall Rating	***			

Chapter 15
GRADING PROGRAMS

Tracking grades and attendance can be an arduous task for faculty. This is especially true for those who assign a wide variety of graded tasks to students every semester such as projects, quizzes, case studies, labs, exams, research papers and the like. When the task is further complicated by adding a variety of relative weighted values to graded assignments, dropping certain exam or quiz grades or giving optional assignments, it is easy to understand why there seem to be so many crabby instructors around grade reporting time at all teaching institutions. While the best grade management program is one custom created by each faculty member to meet his or her exact needs, not all faculty possess the necessary skill to create a truly useful grading system using traditional spreadsheet or database programs. Moreover, many who do possess the requisite skill may lack the time to create the ideal grading program. Fortunately, full-featured grading programs abound. As the two representative software packages reviewed here will show, these feature-packed, highly customizable and useful programs can not only record grades and attendance, but also provide very useful reports and grade analysis that faculty can use to give better feedback to students and to better assess their performance. If you are a faculty member who has reviewed several grading programs in the past five or ten years and found them inadequate, by all means take another look. You will be pleasantly surprised by the changes in these programs.

VAR Grade for Windows 95® Version 2.03

VAR Grade for Windows 95 is one of the most powerful and flexible grading programs available today. The program's look and feel is that of a spreadsheet. Indeed, it duplicates much of what I have been doing for years with my spreadsheet-based grading files without the need to program formulas, define the parameters for graphing data or write any macros. This is not to imply that the process is necessarily simple; complicated grading schemes will still require some, well, complicated setup. But the process is far simpler and less time consuming than developing your own dedicated application from scratch. With a little patience and a willingness to refer to the program's excellent help files, even users with only modest computer literacy skills can create customized grading modules for all of their courses in relatively short order.

The software incorporates a very useful, well implemented tutorial as part of its help system that introduces a new user to the process of creating and using a computerized grading system by providing step-by-step

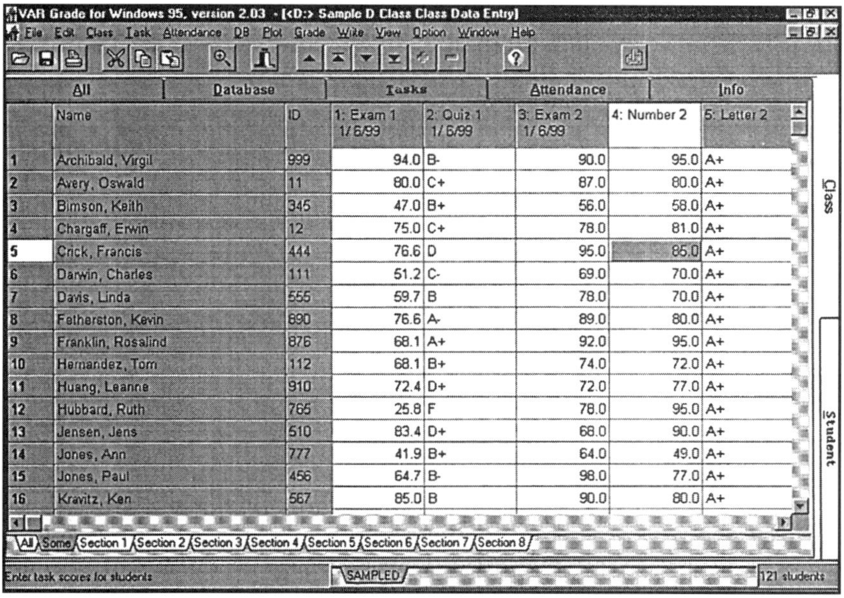

Figure 15.1: VAR Grade for Windows 95 provides the look and feel of a spreadsheet program without requiring complicated programming from the user. Number and letter grades can be freely combined in this program to reflect the instructor's preference. Exporting and importing data to and from other applications is also supported.

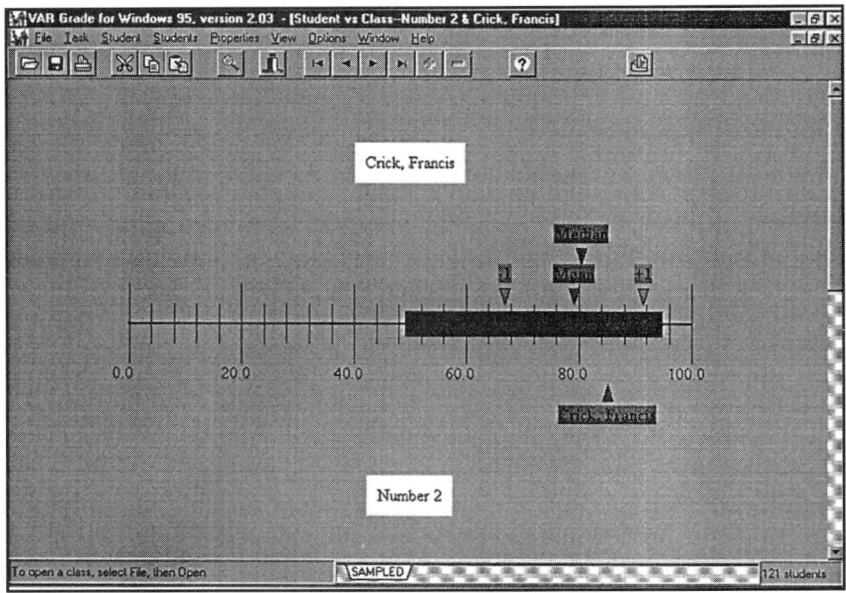

Figure 15.2: Statistical information is readily available. Here, the performance of a single student in relation to the rest of his class on a sample second exam is shown.

instructions and allowing a user to work with included sample files. The program's strong documentation, context-sensitive on-line help and solid tutorials expedite the learning process and ease a new user into full competence with the features of this powerful application program.

VAR Grade for Windows 95 offers exceptional flexibility and adaptability. The program accepts either numerical or letter grades on reported exams, and permits faculty to use any combination of letter and numerical grades to reflect their grading preferences. Dropping low grades, assigning different weight to different tasks, allowing extra-credit or optional assignments and even factoring attendance into a student's final grade are all supported. In addition, the program provides various charting capabilities that can output to the screen or to your printer comparative information about students' performance within a class or between different classes; an individual student's progress throughout the semester can also be tracked graphically, as can his or her performance in comparison to the class as a whole. Useful statistical analysis of student grades is also available, including standard deviation analysis, t-scores, the percentage of students who scored above and below any given student in a class, and students' rank order. Naturally, the program can also performs

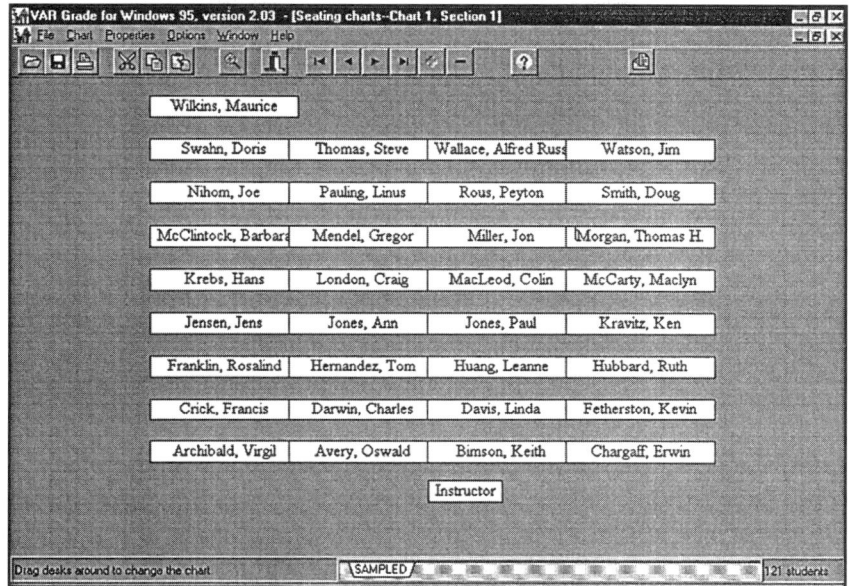

Figure 15.3: *The program can generate charts in random, alphabetized or reverse-alphabetized order. Unfortunately, generating a chart that reflects a student-chosen seating pattern is not readily obtainable.*

more mundane tasks, such as printing progress reports, final grade rosters and individualized grade reports.

In addition to tracking grades, the program can also track and report attendance and even print seating charts. It also allows faculty to leave comments for each student, as well as maintain a database of student contact information such as campus address, phone number and e-mail. In short, unless you're very happy with your current grading system, get an evaluation copy of VAR Grade for Windows 95.

Program Name:	VAR Grade for Windows 95® Version 2.03 ©1997–99
Program Type:	Shareware (expires after 40 uses)
Company Name:	VARed Software
Web Page:	http://www.varedsw.com
E-Mail:	support@varedsw.com *or* varedsw@compuserve.com
Registration Fee:	$45

General Evaluation: VAR Grade for Windows 95 Version 2.03				
	Excellent	*Good*	*Average*	*Poor*
Utility	***			
Ease of Use	***			
Ease of Learning			***	
Documentation	***			
Overall Rating	***			

GradeStar for Windows 95/98/NT® Version 2.2

GradeStar Version 2.2 is another excellent grading program that provides tremendous flexibility with an intuitive user interface. As is true with VAR Grade, mastering GradeStar will require a bit of time and patience. But GradeStar's solid documentation and brief but useful tutorial will make the learning process a generally painless experience. And the benefits offered by this program are well worth the relatively modest investment of time required to master it.

GradeStar allows a user to create an electronic grade book by following some standard steps that include entering the names of students for each class, creating course definitions, creating assignments and exam definitions (and deciding how these will be weighed), entering grades, entering attendance and creating reports. With regard to the key issue of computation of grades, GradeStar provides great flexibility. The program allows graded assignments to be grouped by type, such as exams, quizzes, homework, and the like. Each type of assignment can also be assigned a different weight as a percentage of the total grade. For example, if a course will have a midterm and final, five quizzes, four hourly exams and a term paper, each of these components can be assigned any desired value in computing the final grade, such as 20% for the midterm, 20% for the final, 15% for the quizzes, 15% for the term paper and 30% for the hourly exams. The ability to assign values to groups of assignments by type, rather than only to each individual assignment, is especially useful in cases where instructors assign a variety of graded assignments, as in my last example. Extra-credit assignments and the dropping of lowest grades are also supported. In addition, grades can be assigned either on a percentage or point system (where each assignment is worth a maximum number of points towards the final grade), at the instructor's option.

Chapter 15 : Grading Programs

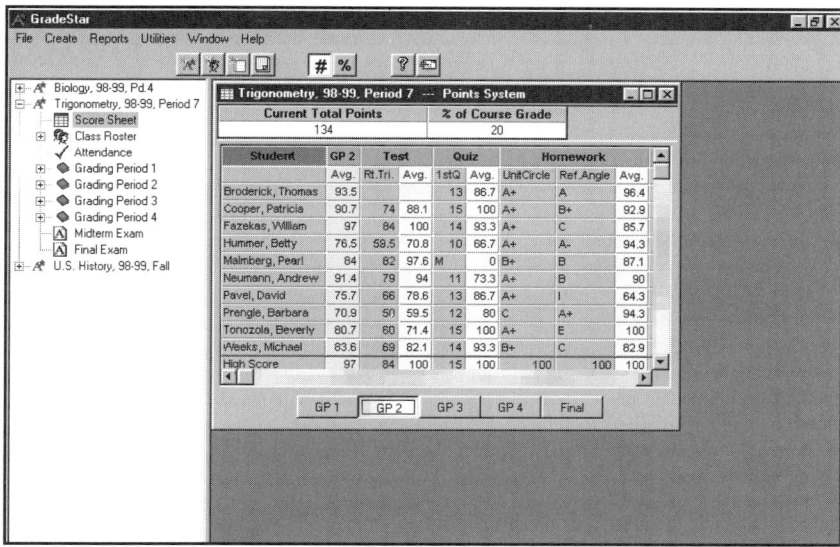

Figure 15.4: GradeStar for Windows 95/98/NT Version 2.2 allows instructors great flexibility in designing customized grade tracking and report generation for all classes taught. Custom reports for any pre-set grading periods can be automatically outputted to the computer screen or to a printer. Separate attendance reports can likewise easily be prepared.

The program also allows for the maintenance of attendance records and the creation of reports for both grades and attendance by class or for each individual student. For the attendance function, the program asks the instructor to select class meeting dates by clicking on a monthly calendar and then generates a class meeting grid into which the instructor may enter attendance information as A (absence), E (excused absence) or T (tardy) for each class meeting date. The information can then be automatically printed for each class and or individual student for any user-selected grading period.

The shareware version of this program is limited only in the number of assignments it allows per grading period (eight) and it does not allow for security features available in the registered version of the program. Otherwise, the shareware version is the same as the registered version of the program, save for the fact that shareware reminder appears for 20 seconds on screen whenever the assignment creation screen is accessed. No time limit on the use of this shareware version of GradeStar is imposed on users.

Although GradeStar does not at present support statistical analysis

112　　　　　　　　　　Unit III : Educational Programs

GradeStar Course Report　　　　　　　　　　1/7/99 2:51:03 PM

Prepared For:　Trial User
Course:　　　　Trigonometry, 98-99, Period 7
Grading Period:　2　　　　　　　Percent Mode

Student	GP 2 Avg.	GP 2 Poss. Pts	GP 2 Ern. Pts	Test Rt.Tri.	Test Avg.	Quiz 1stQ	Quiz Avg.	Homework UnitCircle	Homework Ref.Angle	Homework Avg.
Possible Points	134			84	84	15	15	10	25	35
Date				11/1/98		11/8/98		11/6/98	11/10/98	
Broderick, Thomas	93.5	50	47			86.7	86.7	A+	A	96.4
Cooper, Patricia	90.7	134	122	88.1	88.1	100	100	A+	B+	92.9
Fazekas, William	97	134	130	100	100	93.3	93.3	A+	C	85.7
Hummer, Betty	76.5	134	103	70.8	70.8	66.7	66.7	A+	A-	94.3
Malmberg, Pearl	84	134	112	97.6	97.6	M	0	B+	B	87.1
Neumann, Andrew	91.4	134	123	94	94	73.3	73.3	A+	B	90
Pavel, David	75.7	134	102	78.6	78.6	86.7	86.7	A+	I	64.3
Prengle, Barbara	70.9	134	95	59.5	59.5	80	80	C	A+	94.3
Tonozola, Beverly	80.7	109	88	71.4	71.4	100	100	A+	E	100
Weeks, Michael	83.6	134	112	82.1	82.1	93.3	93.3	B+	C	82.9
High Score	97			100	100	100	100	100	100	100
Low Score	70.9			59.5	59.5	0	0	80	50	64.3

Figure 15.5: Detailed grade and attendance reports can be viewed on-screen (as depicted here) or printed. GradeStar also easily outputs individual student reports and class attendance reports for any selected grading period.

of grades, comparative graphs or charts, or the creation of seating charts, these features, while useful, are by no means essential. With regard to the essential areas of a grading program, GradeStar performs admirably. It is a powerful, flexible, and relatively easy to use program given its powerful features. If you are looking for a grading program, by all means give GradeStar a try.

Program Name:	GradeStar for Windows 95/98/NT® Version 2.2 ©1997—98
Program Type:	Shareware
Company Name:	ShellTech Software Corp.
Address:	P.O. Box 723 Mantoloking, NJ 08738
Web Page:	http://www.shelltech.com
E-Mail:	staff@shelltech.com
Registration Fee:	$49.95 for a single license. (Site licenses are available.)

Chapter 15 : Grading Programs

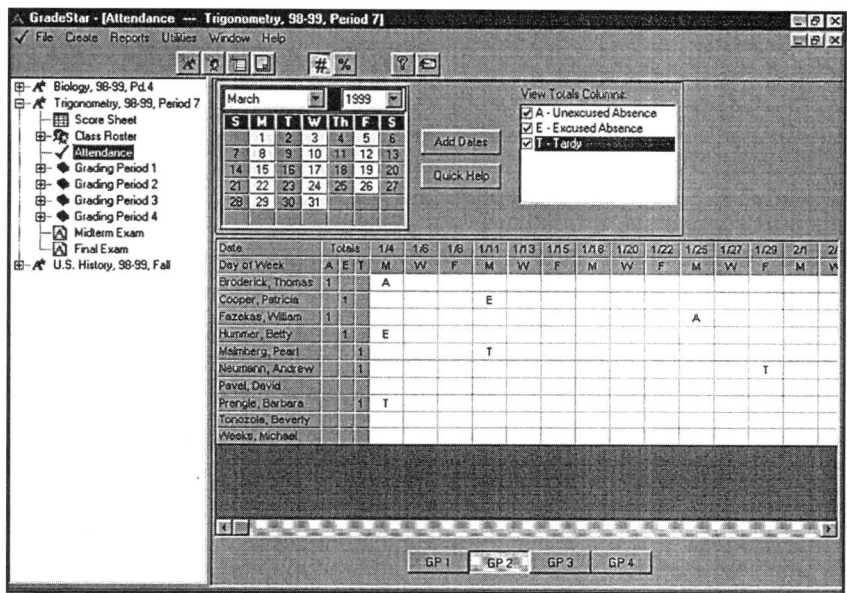

Figure 15.6: Maintaining attendance data for each class is a simple matter. The instructor selects the meeting dates for every class by clicking on the appropriate meeting dates in a monthly calendar, and then dates are then transferred to the attendance grid that accepts A (absent) E (excused absence) and T (Tardy) designations. Attendance reports can be printed along with grade reports for each user-selected grading period.

General Evaluation: GradeStar for Windows 95/98/NT® Version 2.2

	Excellent	Good	Average	Poor
Utility	***			
Ease of Use	***			
Ease of Learning			***	
Documentation	***			
Overall Rating	***			

UNIT IV
INTERNET TOOLS

Since the 1970s, the personal computer has undergone a remarkable evolution from little more than a curiosity and expensive toy for electronic hobbyists, to an ubiquitous, indispensable tool. The steady increase in processing power coupled with a concurrent decrease in price for computers and most peripherals have made computer ownership affordable, while its wide use in business and education has made computer literacy indispensable. One of the indirect benefits of the wide availability of computers to nearly all members of society has been the growth of the worldwide network of computers that make up the Internet. From its modest roots as a loosely knit network of government and education computers intended to maintain the lines of communication open in case of a nuclear attack in the early 1970s, the Internet was used at first primarily by government employees and academics who were part of the privileged few with access to what was at the time prohibitively expensive computer time. In the 1980s, both the running of the computer network that makes up the Internet and its development were turned from federal control to private control. Thus, what was begun as U.S. Department of Defense project quickly turned into a tool embraced and enhanced by the entire world. The Internet's World Wide Web and its ability to transfer hyper linked documents to and from any computer connected to the network anywhere on earth in a matter of seconds, the file transfer protocols that permit easy downloading of files and the free Internet e-mail capabilities made possible by the Internet have arguably had the greatest impact on the dissemination of knowledge since Gutenberg's first printing press.

In this unit, we will explore some of the available shareware and freeware tools that can enhance the capabilities of the Internet and World Wide

Web. I will omit from my discussion the myriad of browser enhancement tools available for Microsoft Explorer and Netscape Communicator because ample information about these related freeware and shareware programs is available from the Microsoft and Netscape web pages (http://www.microsoft.com and http://www.netscape.com), and these supporting programs can be downloaded along with your next upgrade of these browsers. I encourage you to visit both the Microsoft and Netscape pages for the latest upgrade information and to learn more about enhancing your favorite browser's capabilities.

CHAPTER 16
WEB PAGE CREATION

Creating web pages and web documents is a process that many experienced users find cumbersome. For the inexperienced user, the prospect of using Hypertext Markup Language (HTML) to create personal web pages or HTML documents for Web distributing can be an intimidating, frustrating, difficult undertaking. Fortunately, there are many commercial and shareware packages that facilitate the process of creating web pages without having to become an expert in HTML programming. In this chapter, we'll examine a number of web page creation packages available to users that will allow the creation of professional looking web pages.

AOLPress® Version 2.0

Among the available web page creation packages, few are as easy to learn and use as America Online's AOLPress 2.0. The package, aimed at users with limited experience, is not limited to AOL members; any user with the ability to host a web page can use AOLPress to create simple web pages.

The program incorporates an interactive tutorial that combines instruction with hands-on practice, allowing a user to try Web design concepts as soon as they are learned. Creating links, inserting text and graphics, formatting text and graphics, using tables and lists, linking of video and sound files, image mapping and using form handlers are all covered.

Users with limited HTML programming experience who are looking for a relatively fast and easy crash course on web page creation will

118   Unit IV : Internet Tools

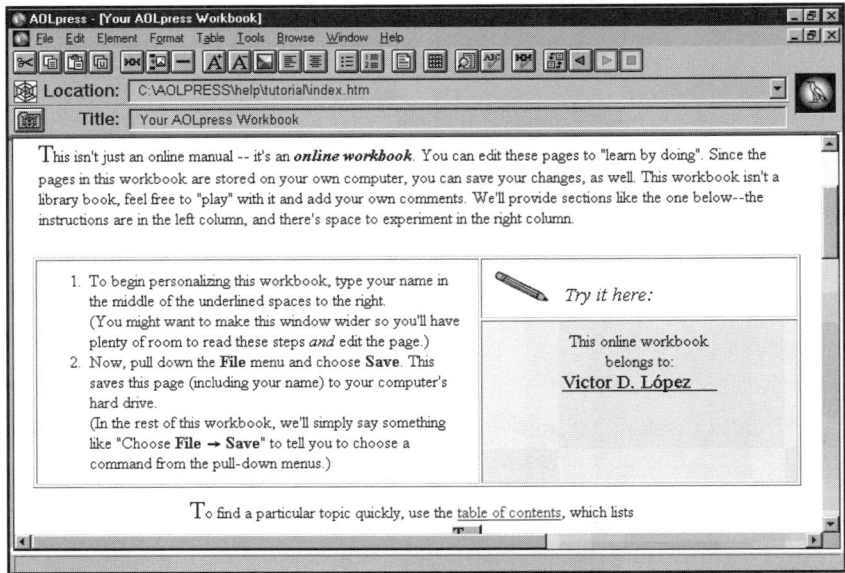

Figure 16.1: AOLPress 2.0 provides a new user with a step-by-step tutorial on building a Web page while teaching the basics of HTML programming.

find little to dislike in this program, especially considering it is available free of cost.

Program Name: AOLPress® Version 2.0 © 1995–97
Program Type: Freeware
Company Name: America Online, Inc.
Company Address: 8619 Westwood Center Drive
Vienna, Virginia 22182
Web Page: http://www.aol.com
Registration Fee: None

General Evaluation: AOLPress Version 2.0

	Excellent	Good	Average	Poor
Utility	***			
Ease of Use		***		
Ease of Learning	***			
Documentation	***			
Overall Rating	***			

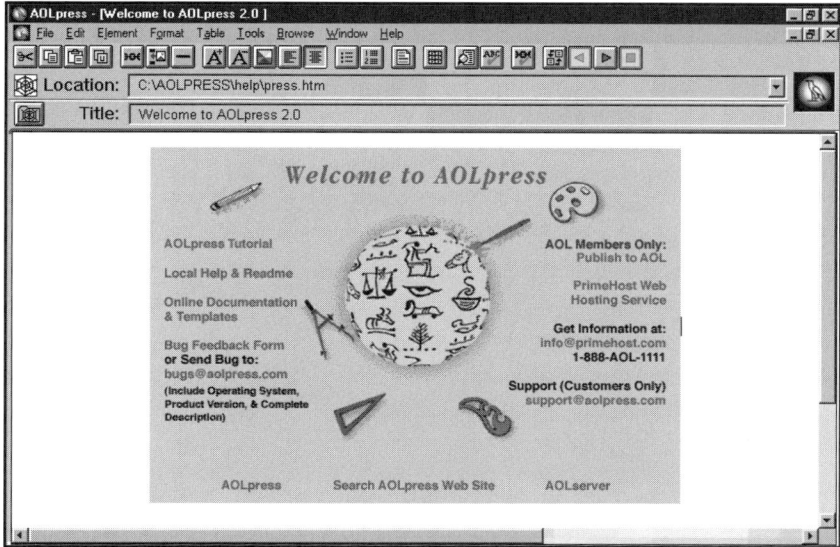

Figure 16.2: AOL Press gives users the opportunity to work off-line or to access on-line documentation and additional help files. In addition, the program provides an excellent menu system and power buttons that facilitate the creation of HTML documents. Once created, users can publish their pages to AOL (if they are members), or to PrimeHost Web Hosting Service. Users can also use FTP to upload their pages to other hosts, such as university or third-party Internet service providers.

Arachnophilia® Version 3.2

Arachnophilia is a web page design program that gives an option of creating HTML documents in one of two ways: importing Rich Text Format (RTF) documents or writing HTML code to create web pages from the ground up. The former method, while more limiting, makes it possible for persons with little HTML programming knowledge or experience to create useful Web documents by using their favorite word processor then saving the document in RTF format. For experienced HTML programmers, the latter method provides the greatest flexibility of design and allows the user to create truly unique, professional web pages limited only by his or her imagination.

Users familiar with HTML programming will appreciate the unobtrusive user interface with customizable power buttons that bring welcomed assistance to most basic programming tasks. Up to eight power button levels can be viewed simultaneously; by clicking on appropriate function

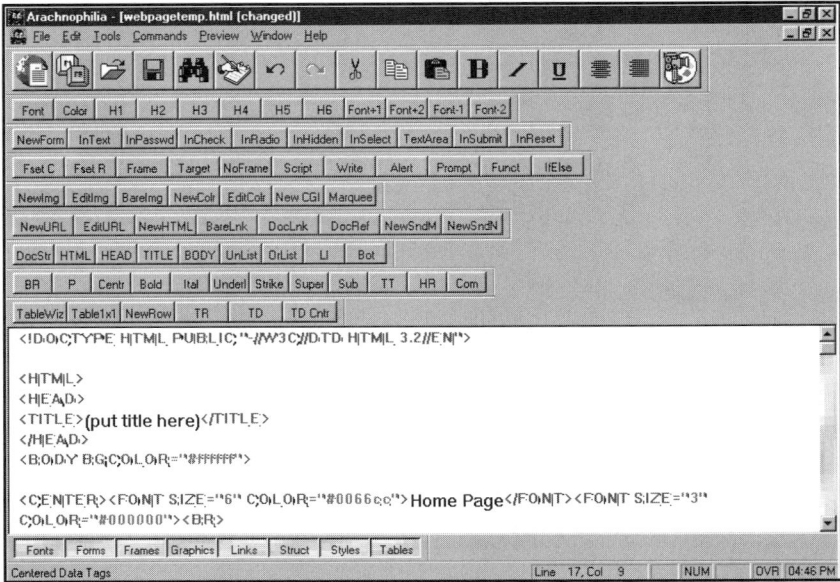

Figure 16.3: *Arachnophilia Version 3.2 provides ample HTML programming assistance through pop-up button bars for eight main functions. A user can select and deselect one or all of these button bars at any time by clicking on the corresponding button at the bottom of the work area. Here, all eight button bars are selected for purposes of illustration—an unlikely choice when using the program.*

type, (See figure 16.3) the user selects one or more button bars from the available function types (Fonts, Forms, Frames, Graphics, Lincs, Structure, Styles and Tables). Power buttons and a full traditional menu interface are also available, along with a useful on-line help system. In addition, context-sensitive help is available at all times via the F1 key. As with other web page design packages, pages can be previewed at any time with your choice of up to six different Web browsers.

Arachnophilia is neither a shareware nor freeware program. Rather, it is being distributed under what its author, Paul Lutus, terms *CareWare*. Rather than asking for payment in money for users of his program, Mr. Lutus asks those who use his program to make a payment by way of effecting a positive change in attitude and behavior. I cannot do credit to his eloquence here, but he essentially requests as payment that users of his program live at least one day as though it were their last, reflecting the kindness towards others, self awareness, empathy, and recognition of the precious, joyous aspects of everyday life we usually fail to appreciate through our limiting attitudes of negativity and pessimism until it is too

Chapter 16 : Web Page Creation 121

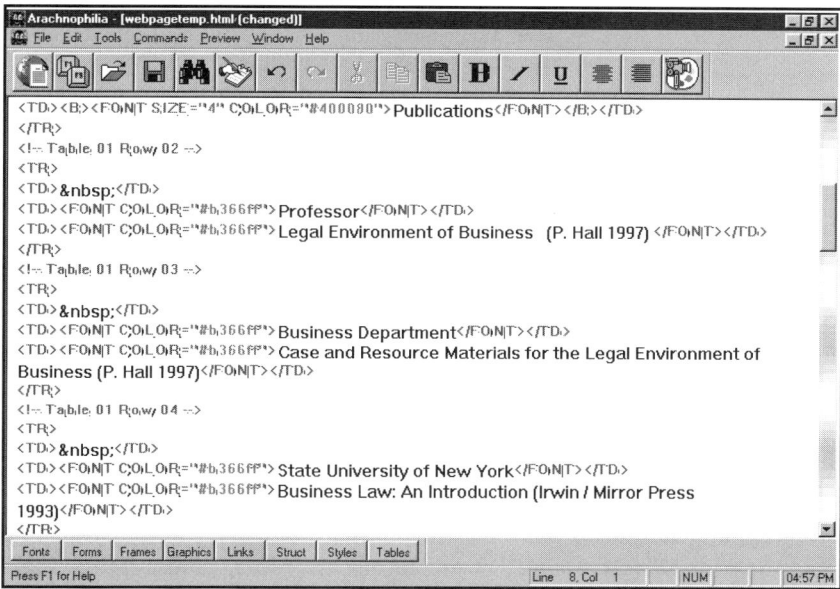

Figure 16.4: Arachnophilia automatically generates HTML code from imported RTF-formatted documents, as in the example above. My tests with several documents showed better results when allowing the program to import and translate RTF files than with merely saving documents in HTML format after their creation with word processing programs. Page formatting and table information were better preserved in the RTF translated documents than by saving these documents in HTML format.

late. Whether or not you love spiders, Web design or this program, I hope you will consider making a payment to the author in his requested coin; it should prove a wise investment with a guaranteed positive return.

Program Name:	Arachnophilia® Version 3.2 © 1996-97
Program Type:	CareWare (No monetary payment is requested.)
Programmer:	Paul Lutus
	Ashland, Oregon
Web Page:	http://www.arachnoid.com
Registration Fee:	None—But view program documentation for CareWare "payment" request. (You may download the most recent version of this program at http://www.arachnoid.com/arachnophelia.)

General Evaluation: Arachnophilia Version 3.2				
	Excellent	Good	Average	Poor
Utility	***			
Ease of Use		***		
Ease of Learning		***		
Documentation	***			
Overall Rating	***			

Tarantula® Release 1.98

Tarantula is a unique web page development program that permits a high degree of flexibility in placing both text and graphic images on a page by dividing the page into areas that can receive formatted text and graphic images. Unlike most HTML editors that merely give users some assistance in writing HTML code via helpful tools, power buttons and menus, Tarantula assists a user in writing the page source code which it then compiles at the end the process. Thus, the program actually generates the necessary HTML code based on the page characteristics selected by the user, a process that greatly simplifies the creation of a web page for the average user. As a result, the program looks and works more like a desk-top publishing package than an HTML editor.

Users who are very competent with HTML programming and who wish to create truly unique pages that reflect their precise tastes and individuality will probably not be happy with this program. But less experienced users who want an off-the-shelf solution for simple web page design without incurring the expense of a leading commercial package such as Microsoft Publisher or Microsoft Front Page will doubtless be pleased with this program's good mix of power and utility.

Tarantula makes it easy to incorporate into a web page design such common features as tables, lists, image mapping, graphics images, and most other features available to HTML programmers. In addition, the program provides enough tools and customizable elements to allow every page designer to differentiate his or her creation from that of others who may use this package to create their personal web pages. Best of all, the program's excellent help system provides helpful hints and context-sensitive help at every step, as well as versatile main menus, keyboard shortcuts, power buttons and context-sensitive menus that are instantly available via a right-click of the mouse.

My only reservation when it comes to this program is its price. At $90 as of this writing, it is priced competitively with the street price of better known commercial products from Microsoft, Corel and others. Still, the product is worth a close look, especially by users unwilling to spend a significant amount of time learning a more powerful package. By all means download a copy of this program and take advantage of Tarantula's 30-day shareware license to put this program through its paces. As always, check the addresses below for current pricing and to obtain the latest release of the program.

Program Name: Tarantula® Release 1.98 © 1998
Program Type: Shareware (30-day license)
Author: Sumit Gupta
Company: Nostrum India
455, Sector A, Pocket C
Vasant Kunj
New Delhi 110 070
INDIA
Web Pages: http://NostrumIndia.com or
http://www.pobox.com/~nostrum
Registration Fee: $90 (For quantity discount information, e-mail discounts@NostrumIndia.com)

General Evaluation: Tarantula Release 1.98

	Excellent	Good	Average	Poor
Utility	***			
Ease of Use	***			
Ease of Learning	***			
Documentation			***	
Overall Rating	***			

CHAPTER 17

WEB BROWSERS

If you are reading this book, chances are you are already intimately familiar with at least one of the two leading Web browsers: Microsoft Explorer or Netscape Communicator. Versions of these two exceptional browsers are available for download free of charge from Microsoft (http://www.microsoft.com) and Netscape (http://www.nescape.com), as well as from other sources. As of this writing, the latest available versions are Netscape Communicator 4.6 and Microsoft Explorer 5.0. Because both Microsoft and Netscape upgrade their browsers regularly, newer versions will most likely be available by the time you read this.

In the browser wars, Netscape's once dominant browser has lost its leadership position to Microsoft's Internet Explorer. How the current federal antitrust suit against Microsoft and America Online's acquisition of Netscape will ultimately impact on Microsoft's current dominance of the browser market is anyone's guess. For the average user, the current competition between browser manufacturers has resulted in two much improved versions of the Microsoft and Netscape browsers as well as a veritable cornucopia of third-party supporting programs that make either browser a top-notch choice for painless Web surfing and e-mail use.

Reviews and side-by-side comparisons of the most popular browsers abound in the popular press. The current crop of these gives Microsoft Internet Explorer the highest marks. But the two browsers are close in features, power and speed. While Internet Explorer currently enjoys the edge over Netscape Communicator, either browser offers exceptional features that will meet the need of most any user from beginner to the most advanced. Having used every version of the Netscape and Microsoft browsers to date, I still use both and find little significant difference between them. Most users who are very familiar with either version of these browsers will find little reason to switch and will probably be best served by upgrading to the latest version of their browser of choice when it becomes available. For new users, I would suggest trying both browsers for several weeks and then choosing the one they are most comfortable with.

It should be noted that the Microsoft and Netscape Web browsers are by no means the only available; other freeware and shareware browsers can be readily found. Given the dominance of these two browsers, their power, flexibility, excellent support and status as de-facto standards, the average user should have no reason to look beyond the two market leaders to find an ideal tool for surfing the Web.

Internet Explorer 5.0®

With Internet Explorer 5.0, Microsoft offers some noteworthy improvements to its popular browser that should continue earning it high marks from average users and professional reviewers alike. Improvements in this version include significantly faster loading of cached pages, a "Search Assistant" to help users find web pages and e-mail addresses, improved look and feel when downloading FTP files (Files and directories look like local files and can be treated much the same way when copying them to a specific location on your disk or directly to your desktop.), enhanced multimedia capabilities, and the ability to seamlessly share files with any other computer using this version of Internet Explorer over the Internet. Windows 95 users will still be able to use the Active Desktop function of Internet Explorer which, in conjunction with installing the Windows 95 service packs available free of charge from Microsoft at its Website, will give users most of the functionality of Windows 98.

On the down side, the improvements to this terrific browser have increased its size to approximately 100 MB (assuming a full install). While this is not a serious detriment given the size of today's hard disk drives, it does pose a problem for users attempting to download the program through modem connections. The process can take hours even at off-peak times, even assuming no annoying disconnections take place. Microsoft will include the browser with the latest release of Windows 98 and, presumably, Windows 2000 when it is released in the (one hopes) not too distant future.

Unit IV : Internet Tools

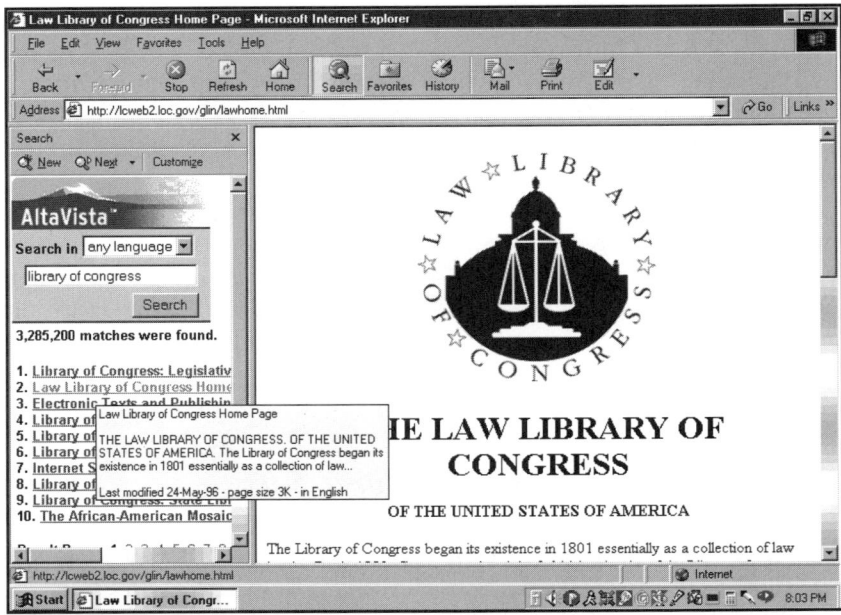

Figure 17.1: A search facility using Alta Vista is available directly from Internet Explorer 5.0 by clicking on the Search button. As illustrated here, the screen is split into sizable frames and a small window momentarily pops up when you move the mouse button over the available choices in the left frame, giving useful information about the site.

Program Name:	Internet Explorer 5.0® © 1995–1999
Program Type:	Freeware
Company:	Microsoft
Web Page:	http://microsoft.com
Registration Fee:	None.

General Evaluation: Internet Explorer 5.0

	Excellent	Good	Average	Poor
Utility	***			
Ease of Use	***			
Ease of Learning	***			
Documentation	***			
Overall Rating	***			

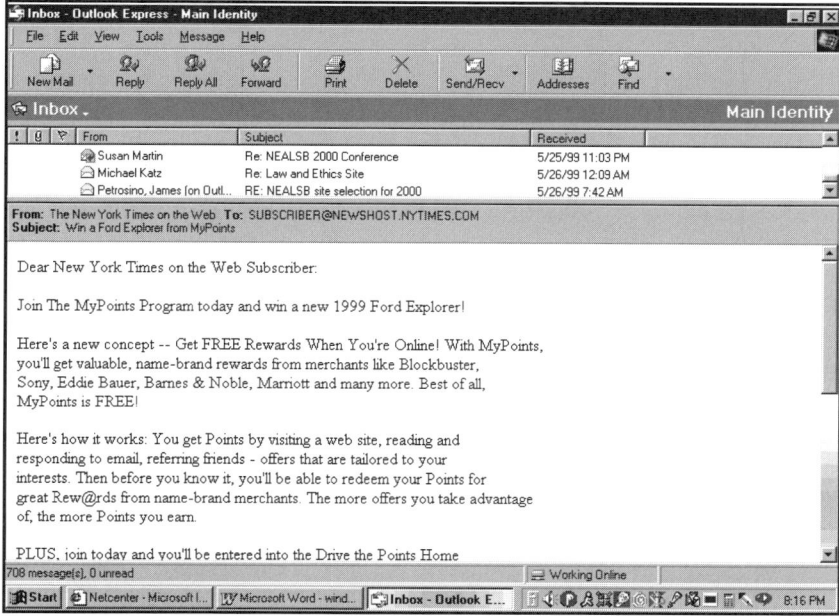

Figure 17.2: Internet Explorer 5.0 can be customized to use your favorite e-mail program. By default, it uses the included Outlook Express program which has enough features to suit most users' needs.

Netscape Communicator 4.6®

Netscape Communicator 4.6 represents the second of two exceptional choices for users who want one of the full-featured, free Web browsers. One of the advantages of using Netscape Communicator over Microsoft's Internet Explorer is the wealth of information and supporting documentation available at Netscape's home page which, in my view at least, offers an advantage for less experienced users who want or need additional documentation, user-friendly support or one-stop shopping for freeware and shareware programs that expand Netscape's impressive built-in capabilities.

As is the case with Internet Explorer, the latest version of Netscape Communicator includes enhancements in performance and reliability along with a variety of features to make navigating the Web faster and easier. Smart Browsing allows Netscape to suggest web sites related to those currently being viewed. NetWatch allows you to select the types of sites you want to be accessible for you and your family. Using the Platform for Internet Content Selection (PICS) standard, NetWatch allows parents to filter out sites unsuitable for their children. AOL's Instant Messenger allows Netscape users to communicate with any American Online user in real time. Netscape has even streamlined the process of downloading Communicator with its SmartUpdate process that allows updating to the latest release of the program without having to download the entire file—a feature that will be very welcomed by users who use a modem to connect to the Internet. In addition, users can select the features and add-on programs they need at the time of downloading their copy of Netscape Communicator, further streamlining the size of the downloaded setup file. Another feature that will be welcomed by users who download large files via modem is Communicator's ability to seamlessly continue interrupted downloads at the point of interruption. Thus, if a 75 MB file download is interrupted after 70 MB have been downloaded due to telephone line problems or communication glitches, Netscape Communicator will allow the download to resume at the point it was interrupted when a connection is reestablished, requiring only the 5 MB of unsaved data to be downloaded, rather than the entire 75 MB file.

Like Internet Explorer, Netscape Communicator offers an entire suite of Internet applications in a single well integrated package. The three modules that make up Netscape Communicator include Navigator (the Web browser), Messenger (a full featured e-mail program) and Composer (an easy to use web page publishing module that allows users to create professional looking web pages without the need to learn HTML programming). The three modules and the AOL Instant Messenger Service can be accessed from Netscape Communicator's main menu.

Program Name: Netscape Communicator 4.6® © 1994—1999
Program Type: Freeware
Company: Netscape
Web Page: http://www.netscape.com
Registration Fee: None.

General Evaluation: Netscape Communicator 4.6

	Excellent	*Good*	*Average*	*Poor*
Utility		***		
Ease of Use		***		
Ease of Learning		***		
Documentation		***		
Overall Rating		***		

UNIT V
GAMES

Perhaps the most popular category of free and user supported software is that of games. This has been the case since the early days of DOS based personal computers and it remains so today. As a group, games are by far the most power hungry of all applications, requiring ever-faster processor speed and graphics acceleration to render the increasingly realistic, highly detailed graphics and rich sound they employ. Thus, while most home and business applications can be run very successfully on a modest entry-level platform, such as an Intel Pentium 200 MMX (or equivalent) processor, such a system is ill equipped to handle the most demanding game applications which, as of this writing, realistically require a minimum of a Pentium II or Pentium III system with a 3D graphics accelerator video card and 64 MB of RAM. By the time the next generation Pentium chip (or its replacement) is available, you can be sure that the first applications to take full advantage of its raw processing power will still be games, driven by the unquenchable thirst of true gamers for an ever-increasingly realistic playing experience that will never be fully satisfied until technology permits a true, full-immersion virtual reality experience with full sensory support. In other words, gamers will not be satisfied until they are literally "in the game," and hardware and software manufacturers will continue to improve games, and the hardware needed to support them, in an attempt to reach this ideal.

The games that appear in the following chapters were selected so as to run with relatively modest equipment. While many of the games in Chapter 18 make full use of 3D video acceleration if it is available, I have omitted games that specifically require it. I do so in order to provide samples of games available for evaluation by users with limited computing resources. In order to be included here, all games must run on systems with 32MB of RAM and an Intel Pentium 200MMX processor. (Most of these will run quite well with as little as 16MB or RAM on at least a Pentium 100 system.) This is well below the current crop of 500+MHZ Pentium III processors that sport a minimum of 64MB of RAM. I've chosen to set the bar low enough so that the vast majority of readers will be able to sample and enjoy these games regardless of how modest their systems might be. For games that appear after Chapter 18, a modest 486 DX 66 or higher computer will run most of them quite nicely. Thus, even users with minimal computing resources will be able to sample and enjoy them without the need to get a second mortgage on the family home!

Finally, I am not unaware that some of the games I have selected for Chapter 18 will be controversial due to their violent nature. Parental discretion in this, as in all things, ought be exercised before children are allowed to sample some of these games. Where violence is a key element of a game, this fact will be clearly noted. I have sampled most of these games for a minimum of two hours prior to writing a review, and some much longer. If they were not engaging, challenging, entertaining and well rendered, they would not have been included here.

CHAPTER 18

ACTION GAMES

First-person perspective arcade-style video games have been enormously popular since they first appeared in the late 1980s. Whether battling German paratroopers, alien monsters or a collection of magical baddies in the classic versions of Wolfenstein 3D, Doom and Hexen respectively, these games share a common theme: kill everything in sight before it has a chance to kill you. Though often attacked for their violent content, these games can be highly entertaining and offer adrenaline-pumping excitement unmatched by any other gaming experience. Whether violence in popular entertainment has a cathartic effect or a desensitizing, coarsening influence on our culture that translates into an increase in real violence is a topic of debate unlikely to be settled in the foreseeable future. Whatever your view on the issue, one thing is clear: none of the games featured in this chapter are suitable for small children. In this, as in all things affecting children, parents should exercise their own discretion. Preview these games first, then decide at what age, if any, you believe your minor children should be allowed to play them.

Doom for Windows 95 Launcher®

The Doom series of 3D action games are DOS-based games. Now a Windows 95 overlay is available that allows them to run in Windows mode and simplifies the setup of sound cards and video graphics cards that sometimes cause resource conflicts when run in DOS native mode under Windows 95/98.

Doom 95 comes with the shareware version of the original DOOM.

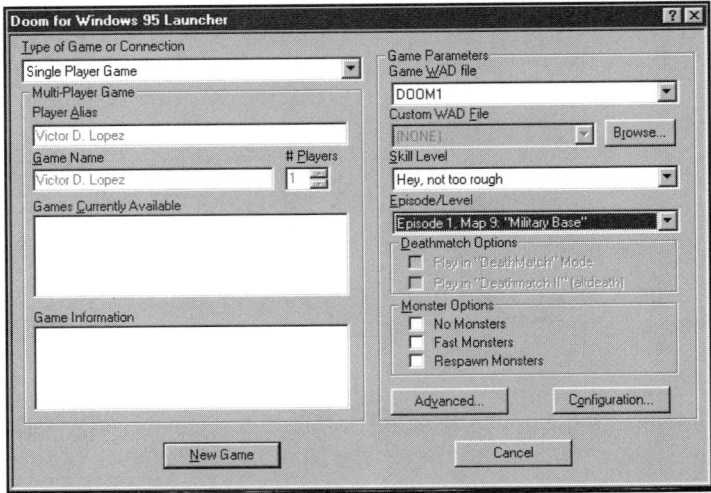

Figure 18.1: *Doom for Windows 95 Launcher simplifies running the DOS-based DOOM programs in Windows 95/98 and allows a user to customize various game features. An especially welcomed feature is the ability to go to a specific level, something even the full versions of DOOM and DOOM II do not permit. Finally, users who own the full versions of DOOM or Wolfenstein 3D can access them all through this overlay program by copying the appropriate WAD files to the same directory into which they install the DOOM for Windows 95 Launcher.*

I've also successfully tested it with the full version of DOOM II and with a shareware version of Wolfenstein 3D, all of which ran successfully. With DOOM II, it cured a resource conflict with my particular PCI sound card that prevented it from being recognized by the game while running in DOS mode.

Doom 95 for Windows 95 Launcher requires very modest system resources (a 486 processor running at 50 MHz or faster with 8 MB or RAM and a VGA video display with at least 256 colors and a Windows 95/98 compatible sound card). Game play over a network is also supported using TCP/IP or SPX/IPX protocols.

The shareware version of DOOM included with this program provides nine levels of progressively difficult play and five difficulty levels from the easy "I'm too young to die" mode to the "Nightmare" level that lives up to its name in the number and types of adversaries with which a player must contend in order to complete each level.

While the graphics and animation are a bit crude when compared to state of the art 3D games such as Quake III, this is still a very playable game that serves as a good introduction into the genre it helped define.

Figure 18.2: The game begins with our hero in perfect health and carrying a revolver with 50 rounds of ammunition. Fortunately, ample weapons can be found throughout various locations during game play, as can medical supplies to regain health after the inevitable barrage of bullets, fireballs, pummeling and bites the game's main character is subjected to almost immediately upon commencing game play. More powerful weapons, including shotguns, chain guns, plasma guns, and rocket launchers, protective armor and ammunition can also be found scattered about and hidden behind walls throughout the various buildings involved in the game play. Less experienced players with a poor sense of direction (such as this writer) will find comfort in the available map function that shows a player's current location as well as all visited areas in the current level any time the TAB key is pressed.

Program Name:	DOOM for Windows 95 Launcher® 1995
Program Type:	Commercial Demo
Company Name:	id Software, Ltd.
Telephone:	(800) IDGAMES (orders only)
Web Page:	http://www.idsoftware.com
Registration Fee:	None (The commercial version of DOOM II, this game's sequel, is available from id Software and software retailers.)

General Evaluation: DOOM for Windows 95 Launcher

	Excellent	Good	Average	Poor
Level of Challenge	***			
Ability to Maintain Interest		***		

Unit V : Games

	Excellent	Good	Average	Poor
Graphics and Sound		***		
Ease of Learning	***			
Documentation	***			
Overall Rating	***			

Hexen II®

Hexen II is another in a series of best selling 3D action games from id Software. As in all games of this type, the purpose is to stay alive, a task generally completed by decimating as many enemies as possible while gathering weapons, solving puzzles and advancing from level to ever-increasingly difficult level. A haunting musical track and beautifully detailed graphics enhance the game playing experience as you do battle

Figure 18.3: As with DOOM and other first-person perspective games, we see only what the character sees as he readies for battle. Here, the Paladin's sword is visible to the right of the screen as he approaches a knight archer for hand-to-hand combat. The lower portion of the screen displays vital information about the game, including the protagonist's current health level and the special artifacts in his inventory that he can access by pressing the enter key. (The torch, displayed here, will allow him to light up dark places. Other useful items include health elixirs, tomes of power that enhance the player's weapons for a time, invisiblity sphere, and many others.)

Figure 18.4: Force alone will not win the day. Sometimes hidden objects can hold the key to success or even objects in plain sight that may need to be used in an unusual way. Here, our hero stands on a catapult that he must use to propel himself over battlement walls. He will suffer some damage from a rough landing, but will live to fight on.

with armies of warriors and magical creatures that include knight archers, spiders, scorpions, fallen angels, hydras, golems, wizards, medusas, ware jaguars and other mythical and quasi human opponents than can be conjured up in the most imaginative of our nightmares.

The game can be played from the first-person perspective of one of four heroic protagonists: crusader, paladin, assassin and necromancer. Each protagonist has strengths and weaknesses that must be taken into account in developing a successful game strategy. The crusader is a holy man and healer who employs powerful mystical weapons and possesses the ability to take punishment well, aided by his power of self-healing. The paladin is a powerful warrior who can muster great strength and skill in hand-to-hand combat; he also possesses some magical abilities, including the power to swim effortlessly and, with the possession of the appropriate relic, the power of flight. The assassin is a stealthy opponent far more circumspect in her fighting abilities than the first two heroes; she relies primarily on her abilities to strike when her victims least expect it, aided by her quickness, stealth and near invisibility to her foes. The necromancer employs magical weapons and obtains power from collecting the souls of his defeated foes; though physically weak, his power is devastating and most effective when employed to kill his foes from a distance.

The game supports both stand-alone and multi player gaming. Limited on-line help is available, and the demo version of the game includes an HTML file that provides technical support information as well as a wealth of well written background information on the general game scenario that will enhance the enjoyment of the gaming experience by placing the action in a well developed fictional context. It is noteworthy that the excellent graphics and smooth-scrolling animation involved in the game are achieved without the need for premium hardware. The minimum system requirements are a very modest Pentium 90 MHZ system with 16 MB of RAM, a sound card and 120 MB of uncompressed disk space. (Preferred requirements are also quite modest: a minimum of a Pentium 120 MHZ system with 24 MB of RAM.)

Program Name: Hexen II® 1996, 1997
Program Type: Commercial Demo
Company Name: id Software, Inc.
Telephone: (800) IDGAMES (orders only)
Web Page: http://www.idsoftware.com
Registration Fee: None (The commercial version of the game is available directly from id Software and through software retailers.)

General Evaluation: Hexen II

	Excellent	Good	Average	Poor
Level of Challenge	***			
Ability to Maintain Interest	***			
Graphics and Sound	***			
Ease of Learning	***			
Documentation	***			
Overall Rating	***			

Duke Nukem 3D®

Apogee Software, Ltd., founded in 1987, was one of the pioneers in the shareware marketing field with popular action games that included the

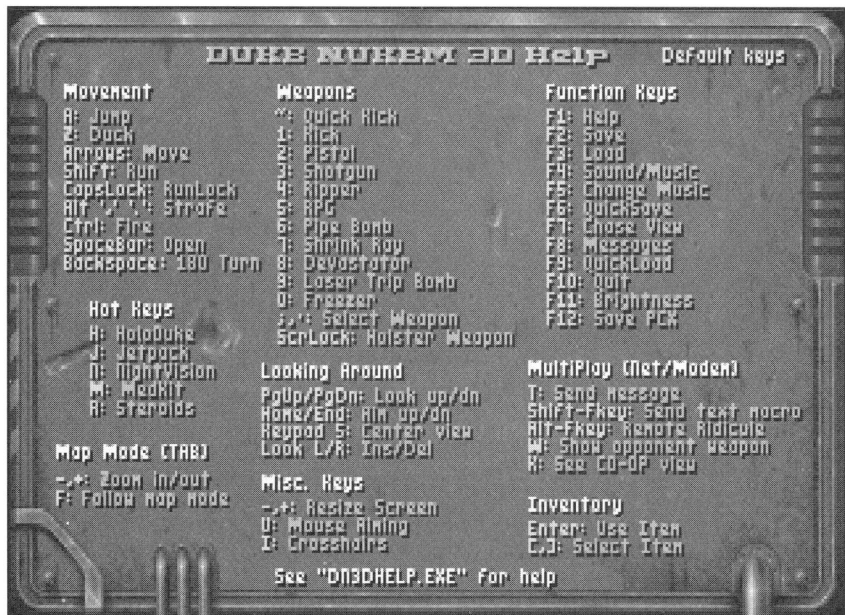

Figure 18.5: Duke Nukem 3D offers help via a help screen, shown here, as well as a 31 page printable text file.

classic games Beyond the Titanic, Kroz, Commander Keen, Pharaoh's Tomb and the original Duke Nukem, along with nearly two dozen others. In 1994, Apogee created 3D Realms Entertainment as a new division devoted to creating and marketing interactive and 3D action games. In early1996, Duke Nukem 3D was first released as shareware, with the full commercial product following shortly thereafter, and quickly became a best selling game, and one of the most downloaded shareware title in this genre.

Aside from terrific graphics and music, the game offers a high level of realism and, though quite violent in nature, the game's virtual gore is tempered with humor. Anthropomorphized minions of quasi human beasts with a taste for killing humans, watching go-go dancers and skin flicks, make hearty opponents that one can't quite take too seriously. Shoot an exotic dancer (I did, by mistake) and they turn into monsters; leave them alone and they're quite harmless.

Large locales with indoor and outdoor action, armies of cunning enemies and interesting puzzles to solve on the way to completing each level make Duke Nukem 3D more challenging than most games in this genre. Likewise, the weapons and ammunition found throughout the game will

Figure 18.6: *Realistic locales, smooth animation and attention to detail are clearly evident. Here, a character is half spun around by taking a direct shotgun blast, as blood momentarily splatters. A moment later, he will continue to advance and shoot, requiring at least one more shot prior to being killed. Some enemies will crouch and drop to the ground while continuing to fire, making them even harder to hit. The bottom portion of the screen provides typical information on Duke Nukem's health, armor, available weapons and ammunition, special artifacts he may be carrying and the available keys, crucial to opening locked doors or operating machinery, that he has found and is currently holding.*

not be available in all levels. After completing level two with a nice cache of weapons, Duke Nukem materializes into a very dangerous situation in level three without any weapon, leaving him to kick his first opponent to death in order to recover a weapon with very few bullets. Even in the second of four levels of play (Piece of Cake, Let's Rock, Come Get Some and I'm Good), it is very difficult to successfully complete level three, even with liberal usage of the game save option. The shareware version of the game contains six full levels; more levels are available with the full registered version, as well as two additional full episodes.

The violence and mild adult content in this game makes it unsuitable for younger players. The minimum system requirements for this game are quite modest: a 486 DX 66 with at least 8MB of RAM. A Pentium system with at least 16 MB of RAM is recommended.

Program Name:	Duke Nukem 3D® 1996
Program Type:	Shareware
Company Name:	3D Realms Entertainment
Telephone:	1-800-3DREALMS (orders only)
Web Page:	http://www.apogee1.com
Registration Fee:	Call 3D Realms Entertainment or visit Apogee's home page for current direct pricing. This game and other 3D Realms Entertainment titles are also available through software retailers.

General Evaluation: Duke Nukem 3D

	Excellent	Good	Average	Poor
Level of Challenge	***			
Ability to Maintain Interest	***			
Graphics and Sound	***			
Ease of Learning	***			
Documentation	***			
Overall Rating	***			

Quake II®

When it was first released in 1996, Quake II immediately gained accolades from reviewers and gaming aficionados for its superb graphics and realistic game play. Three years later, its place among the finest ever first-person perspective 3D action games is undiminished. The three level shareware version of the game is still one of the most popular downloads notwithstanding the hours it can take to download this 38 MB program. As of this writing, a pre-release beta version of Quake III is available for review, but I've decided not to include it here because it requires a 3D graphics accelerator board and a *fast* Pentium II or III system for tolerable game play. Indeed, the Quake II trial version is only tolerably playable on low-end Pentium systems other than in a fairly small windowed mode approximately one third the normal full-screen size (e.g., 400 X 300 video mode). In full screen mode, the game will be quite choppy on low-end systems. The game's stated minimum requirements of a Pentium 90 with 16 MB of RAM (Pentium 133 recommended) are rather optimistic, to say the least; game play on a Pentium 200 MMX system with 40 MB of RAM and 2 MB (non 3D) graphics accelerator board is barely adequate in full screen mode, with noticeable choppiness as the graphics card and slower

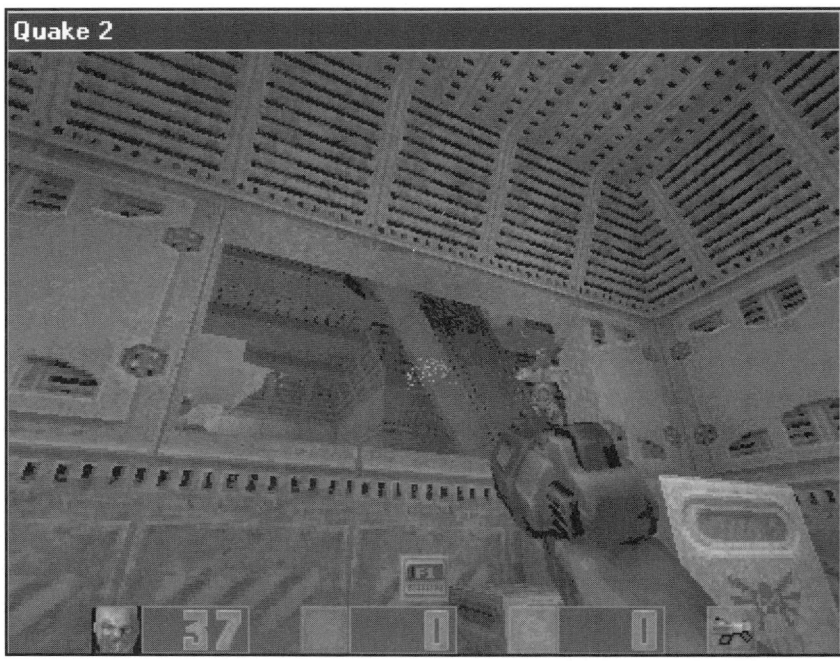

Figure 18.7: *Game play in Quake II is made quite challenging by the need to aim at opponents while they zigzag, crouch and have little trouble shooting at you. In a situation such as this, where you must shoot at an enemy shooting at you from above, the task is not an easy one. Unlike most games of this nature, targeting is not an automatic function; you can't simply shoot in the general area of an opponent with the computer guiding the shot to its target, but must aim the shot close to the opponent in order to score a hit. And the tougher opponents will require many hits before dying, especially from the lower-grade sidearm depicted here.*

processor struggle to keep up with the richly detailed graphics and sound the game provides. To truly appreciate this game in full screen mode requires a Pentium II class processor and 3D graphics acceleration. If you have a Pentium II class system or better with 3D graphics acceleration, download the Quake III test directly from id Software (http://www.idsoftware.com) or one of the many mirror sites that carry the game. By the time you read this, a new release with bug fixes and better 3D graphics support will be available.

In addition to a richly detailed visual and sound environment, the game provides tough opponents who fight uncannily well and, for the most part, require multiple hits to kill from most of the available weapons in the player's arsenal. Opponents will zig-zag towards you while firing

Figure 18.8: *Fighting multiple foes simultaneously can be quite a challenge, especially when they fire their weapons and rush you to inflict greater damage at close range. Having the right weapon in hand with ample ammunition helps, but taking a moment to switch to the appropriate weapon in mid battle can prove deadly, as your powerful, cunning opponents leave precious little room for error and will capitalize on your every mistake or momentary hesitation. On the other hand, some of the monsters will sometimes fight against one another; at such times, you can hide in the background and wait for them to vanquish or weaken each other before taking them on.*

their weapons and will crouch when shot at. As a result, winning this game demands more tactical skill and planning than the common task of shooting in the general direction of an opponent in most games of this nature. Eradicating the hordes of powerful, resilient, cunning and well-armed adversaries with the limited resources at a player's disposal is not an easy task. The test version of Quake II does not allow the changing of difficulty setting, but the full version can be played in one of four levels of difficulty: easy, medium, hard and nightmare. Unlike most games of this type, killing an opponent does not yield extra (unspent) ammunition. Necessary ammunition for the various types of weapons must be found scattered around the game area in the usual caches. Conservation of ammunition and judicious choice in weapons selection is essential to successful completion of this demo.

The level of violence in this game is high; I would rate it unsuitable for players under the age of 17 without parental consent. That aside, Quake II is an engaging, challenging action game that will provide a thoroughly immersive experience. Completing the three-level trial version of this game will challenge even very experienced players the first time it is played, and will provide nearly as much of a challenge the second time around.

Program Name: Quake II® 1997
Program Type: Demo
Company Name: id Software, Inc.
Telephone: (800) IDGAMES (orders only)
Web Page: http://www.idsoftware.com
Registration Fee: None. (Check with id Software for current pricing. The commercial version of the game is also available through software retailers.)

General Evaluation: Quake II

	Excellent	Good	Average	Poor
Level of Challenge	***			
Ability to Maintain Interest	***			
Graphics and Sound	***			
Ease of Learning	***			
Documentation	***			
Overall Rating	***			

Outlaws®

Outlaws is a first-person perspective shoot-em-up game by Lucas Arts Entertainment Company. The game offers a distinctive Old West flavor with excellent cartoon-like graphics, music and realistic sound effects that include frequent verbal taunts and threats.

The background for this game is simple: you play the part of former Marshal James Anderson on a mission to retrieve your daughter, who has been kidnapped by an evil land baron. Your quest takes you to an Old West town full of evil gunslingers whom you must (not surprisingly) kill. Your opponents are wily, good shooting nasties, especially the ones wearing red shirts who shoot fast and will take several hits before dying.

Figure 18.9: *The bottom portion of the screen provides vital information such as bullets left in the current weapon (two are shown to the left of the number 18, the number of bullets in your gun belt) and your current health, represented by the cards with the heart symbols on the lower right portion of the screen. Eating pies you find along the way improves your health, as does a harder to find health elixir, while picking up bullets for the gun or rifle and shotgun shells replenish your supply of these valuable commodities. Reloading is important, too. Pressing the "R" key on the keyboard results in bullets being inserted into the gun's chamber one at a time, a process that takes valuable time. Reloading in the middle of a gunfight is hazardous to your health.*

While somewhat less graphically violent than the other games reviewed in this chapter (some blood will be evident when the bad guys are shot, but no splattering of blood or body parts flying about the screen when hit by grenades, rocket launchers or exploding barrels of toxic waste as is the case in DOOM, Quake II and Duke Nukem 3D), there is no shortage of death and dying here, though the violence is more reminiscent of Saturday morning cartoons than R-rated action films. If I were to rate this game based on the familiar motion picture standards, I would rate it as PG-13.

The game can be played on one of three levels: good, bad and ugly (I wonder if Clint Eastwood would approve?). Even in the "good" level, clearing the town of all the bad guys (no, there are no women gunslingers

Figure 18.10: *Once you find the rifle and the rifle scope, you can shoot your opponents from a relatively safe distance by zeroing in on them through the scope. No need to adjust for distance in your aiming; you will always hit whatever is in the cross hairs, regardless of the distance of your target. On the other hand, using the scope makes aiming a slower process, so having outlaws pop in unexpectedly when you have your scope on can be dangerous. Fortunately, the scope can be mounted and removed quickly by pressing the number 3 on your keyboard. You can always select any available weapon by pressing its assigned number (e.g., fists 1, gun 2, rifle/scope 3, shotgun 4). The shotgun at close range is particularly devastating, but reloading after each shot slows you down.*

in this game) is quite a challenging task. The "bad" level raises the stakes by throwing more bad guys at our hero while making him less resistant to being shot. The "ugly" level has even more outlaws and even less resistance by part of Marshal James to their fire power. Regardless of the level chosen, you will have at your disposal essentially four weapons: your fists, a six shooter, a repeating rifle with a "detachable" scope and a single-shot shotgun; the last two weapons are available once they are found during game play. If you can find it, dynamite will also be available for use. As is the norm for games of this type, ammunition for all three guns can be found scattered about, and gun belts containing unused bullets for the revolver can sometimes be retrieved from killed outlaws.

The cartoon-like characters in this game have distinct personalities and feature realistic motion. Some innocent townsfolk are scattered around in key places during game play. Shoot them by accident, and they will die. Outlaws will sometimes seem to hide behind them when shooting at you, but for the most part the nervous-looking townspeople and innocent store clerks mill about trying to stay out of harm's way.

The demo version of this game features a single level consisting of the various buildings in the town. Hidden areas and multiple-story structures are featured, and useful objects must be retrieved in order to access certain parts of the town (e.g., keys must be found before locked doors can be opened). Once every room in every building has been rid of outlaws, a process that takes an appreciable amount of time, one final bad guy appears who is the hardest to kill of all. Vanquish him, and the level is done. To save Marshal James' daughter you'll need to buy the full version of the game, though, as the adventure continues.

The full version of Outlaws allows for single user or network play. The demo version of Outlaws I reviewed allows only single user play, but a multi-player patch is available at the LucasArts home page. The minimum system requirements for this game demo are indeed quite modest: a Pentium 60 MHz system with 16 MB of RAM, a 16 bit sound card, and an SVGA graphics card and monitor, in addition to Windows 95/98. I did sample this game in a mothballed system with only the minimal requirements and it actually played quite well in full screen mode. That was a nice surprise. (Don't try that with Quake II, or even Duke Nukem!) At a relatively modest 13.5 MB in its compressed downloaded file format that installs onto approximately 30 MB of hard disk space, this demo can be downloaded fairly comfortably with a 56K modem, or even an old 28K modem, if time is not of the essence for you.

Program Name:	Outlaws® 1997
Program Type:	Demo
Company Name:	LucasArts Entertainment Company
Address:	P.O. Box 14797 Fremont, CA 94539
Telephone:	1-888-LEC-GAMES (orders only)
Web Page:	http://www.lucasarts.com
Registration Fee:	None. (Check with LucasArts Entertainment Company for current pricing. The commercial version of the game is also available through software retailers.)

General Evaluation: Outlaws

	Excellent	Good	Average	Poor
Level of Challenge	***			
Ability to Maintain Interest	***			
Graphics and Sound	***			
Ease of Learning	***			
Documentation	***			
Overall Rating	***			

CHAPTER 19

ARCADE-STYLE GAMES

Before dedicated game machines and personal computers made video games popular and accessible, video arcades were a popular, fun place for youngsters, young adult and the young at heart to congregate. To be sure, these establishments still exist today, but they have lost much of the special charm they held when they were the only place where, for a quarter, you could save the earth from hordes of unfriendly aliens from other planets, help a hapless frog across traffic into the safety of his lily pad, or pilot your jet fighter into enemy territory. To be sure, some of the early games were crude, by today's standards (would anyone pay a quarter today to play Pong?). But they were, nevertheless, a source of good, clean, escapist fun. In this chapter, we'll look at some modern remakes of old classics as well as new offerings from the fertile imaginations of programmers who can still engage our interest and make us yearn to see our names in the high score list.

Alien Ambush®

Alien Ambush is a space shoot-'em-up game somewhat evocative of the classic Space Invaders arcade game. The object of the game is to rid two sectors of space at a time of attacking aliens. After ridding two sectors (game screens) of aliens, it is time to rejoin the mother ship for refueling, a process that requires successful navigation of an asteroid field, before taking on the next two waves of alien attacks.

Updated music and nine types of enemy aliens (ranging from 100–900

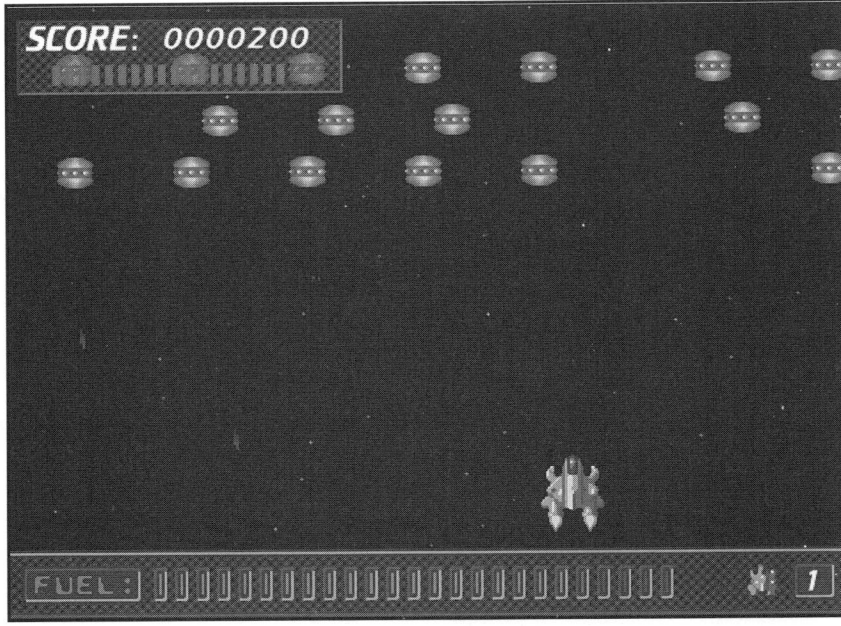

Figure 19.1: *Ridding the universe of the first wave of attacking aliens is quite easy, but succeeding waves of aliens are much harder to dispatch. Refueling between missions is also no easy task.*

points each in value) make this a fun test of hand-eye coordination. Keyboard, mouse and joystick play are all supported. While simple in concept and easy to play, this game is by no means easy to win.

Fans of first generation arcade games will enjoy this new variation on an old theme without the need to carry around pockets full of quarters.

Program Name:	Alien Ambush® 1997
Program Type:	Demo
Company:	The SGN/Starline Company
Telephone:	1-800-699-6395 (orders only)
Web Page:	http://www.nstarsolutions.com
Registration Fee:	$12 for the full version of the game

General Evaluation: Alien Ambush				
	Excellent	*Good*	*Average*	*Poor*
Level of Challenge		***		
Ability to Maintain Interest		***		
Graphics and Sound		***		
Ease of Learning	***			
Documentation	***			
Overall Rating		***		

Ant Run Pro®

Ant Run Pro is an extremely entertaining and challenging game that requires not only quick reflexes but also solid problem solving skills. The object of the game is simple: arrange the random pieces of ant tunnels in every game board in such a way as to facilitate the passage of an ant from one area in the anthill to another. The longer you can interconnect pieces of tunnel together to facilitate the ant's progress, the higher the score. Clicking on each of 48 available tiles with the left mouse button causes them to rotate 90 degrees, thereby allowing the randomly generated tiles with straight and bent pieces of tunnel to be fitted together into a continuous pathway for the ant to travel.

The game is loosely based on the same concept as Pipe Dreams, the commercial game from LucasArts, and other similar games in which the object is to connect scrambled pieces of pipes together to facilitate the flow of water or oil. But the game offers more than a mere variation on a theme. At the beginning of every game, a window pops up with facts about ants, accompanied by verbal cues and a catchy musical score. Fitting together the random pieces of tunnel to keep the ant moving for the minimum time required in order to advance from one level to the next is no easy task. Quick thinking is crucial to maximize the length of the tunnel and to contrive its extension from one corner of the game board to the next (the ant will emerge at the opposite end of the game board from where it exits when it hits the board's edge). And sections of the tunnel are removed once the ant passes through them, making it harder and harder to continue the tunnel's progress until enough time elapses that the next level of tunnel pieces materialize on the game board.

The randomness of tunnel piece placement makes mastering this game a difficult task even after repeated play. Unlike too many arcade games

Figure 19.2: *Once an ant has traversed the tunnels you connect for it from its random starting point anywhere in the playing field, the pieces disappear from the board (the blank areas here with no tunnel pieces represent places through which the ant has already traveled). In the example shown here, when the ant reaches the edge of the playing board at the third tile from the bottom left, it will not be able to emerge at the opposing end of the playing field, an area it has already traversed, and the game will end. A combination of quick thinking, fast reflexes and luck in the original placement of tunnel pieces are all essential for advancing in this very challenging and engaging game.*

that exercise only your trigger finger, this game will make you flex your mental muscles as well. System requirements: Windows 95/98 and 16 MB of RAM.

Program Name:	Ant Run Pro® 1999
Program Type:	Shareware
Company:	Soleau Software, Inc.
Telephone:	212-721-2361
Web Page:	http://www.soleau.com
Registration Fee:	$18 plus $3 shipping/handling (Quantity discounts available.)

Figure 19.3: *The beginning of every game presents a new interesting fact about ants such as that shown here.*

General Evaluation: Ant Run Pro				
	Excellent	*Good*	*Average*	*Poor*
Level of Challenge		***		
Ability to Maintain Interest		***		
Graphics and Sound		***		
Ease of Learning		***		
Documentation		***		
Overall Rating		***		

Pharaoh's Ascent® Version 1.4.2

Pharaoh's Ascent combines arcade action, albeit at a slow, thoughtful pace, with a series of challenging puzzles for a thoroughly enjoyable experience.

The basic aim of the game is to have you help a pharaoh's soul arise out of his pyramid in order to take its proper place in the heavens. The

Figure 19.4: *Typical puzzle in Pharaoh's Ascent, where our hero needs to find a way to get the Ankh, resting on slabs of stone above him (top center), to fall to the keyhole (bottom center) immediately below it. The lighter blocks can be destroyed or tunneled through, but not the darker granite. Removing or moving blocks (or sections of the pillars below) to have the Ankh fall into place, without destroying the Pharaoh's soul (yes, his soul can be destroyed if the Ankh or a slab fall on it from a sufficient height) is not as easy a task as it might first appear. This game will leave you yearning for the full version's 91 levels when you complete the demo's seven levels.*

means for doing so will require that you solve a series of challenging puzzles that will allow him to open and access the exit out of a series of 91 rooms (seven of which are playable in this demo version of the game, the first of which runs automatically to let you see the room's solution and give you an idea of how to approach game play). Most of the solutions are not immediately obvious and will require some planning and time to complete. Adding insult to injury, the gods will take pity on you if you are unable to work through the solution to any level within 15 minutes and will offer you their assistance by means of hints as to the puzzle's solution that you can accept or reject. If enough time passes, more assistance is offered. The basis for all of the puzzles centers around having to figure out a means of having a pharaoh-sized Ankh rolled onto a keyhole in order to open the exit to each room that the pharaoh may then go through. Moving walls and columns and tunneling through wall sections will all be required in the process of liberating the pharaoh's soul. Fortunately, the pharaoh's soul is strong and has the ability to emit ball lightning from his staff on command, a handy tool that can destroy sections of walls, roll an Ankh from a distance, and deal with some of the unhelpful denizens that reside in some of the pyramid's rooms. Levels (rooms) can be restarted at any point or exited prior to their completion.

Players who crave fast action and frenzied game play will need to look elsewhere. Those who prefer cogitation to perspiration, however, will find a winner in this well rendered, challenging, and thoroughly absorbing game.

Program Name:	Pharaoh's Ascent Version 1.4.2® 1997
Program Type:	Demo
Company:	Ambertec, Inc.
Address:	Pharaoh's Ascent Sales P.O. Box 61345 Sunnyvale, CA 94088-1345
Telephone:	1-800-551-6979 (orders only)
E-mail:	sales@ambertec.com
Registration Fee:	None. The price for the full version is $29.95 + $4.50. (Check for current pricing.)

General Evaluation: Pharaoh's Ascent Version 1.4.2

	Excellent	*Good*	*Average*	*Poor*
Level of Challenge		***		
Ability to Maintain Interest		***		
Graphics and Sound		***		
Ease of Learning		***		
Documentation		***		
Overall Rating		***		

X-Wing Alliance Demo® Version 1.00

Fans of Star Wars and flight combat simulators will find much to like in the demo version of LucasArts X-Wing Alliance. The game offers one playable training mission that will provide a good overview of the excellent graphics, sound effects and music this space combat simulation game offers.

Figure 19.5: This graphic snapshot does not do justice to the slick, highly detailed graphics the game offers. It is offered here only to give a rough idea of the straight ahead battle console from the game. As with most other games that use DirectX, sharp screen captures with the Print Screen key or most of the available graphics capture programs yield poor results.

The training mission is not an easy one to complete, even for players familiar with flight simulators or space combat games. Enemy ships are fast, cunning and deadly accurate, and locking onto them for a kill is no easy task. Game play adheres to the old adage that combat is controlled chaos. Two radar displays in the upper left and upper right portions of your screen show enemy and friendly craft at your 12:00 o'clock and 6:00 o'clock positions. Looking out for enemy craft on your tail while attempting to engage enemy craft directly ahead requires constant scanning of the screen and radar, and enemy avoidance and pursuit demands good throttle and flight stick control, as well as judicious use of lasers and missiles, for survival.

Minimum system requirements for this game include a Pentium 200 processor running Windows 95/98 with 32 MB of RAM and a 2 MB PCI card. Microsoft DirectX support is also required, as is the case for many of the graphics-intensive games. (If you do not already have a version of DirectX loaded, you can readily download the latest drivers from most

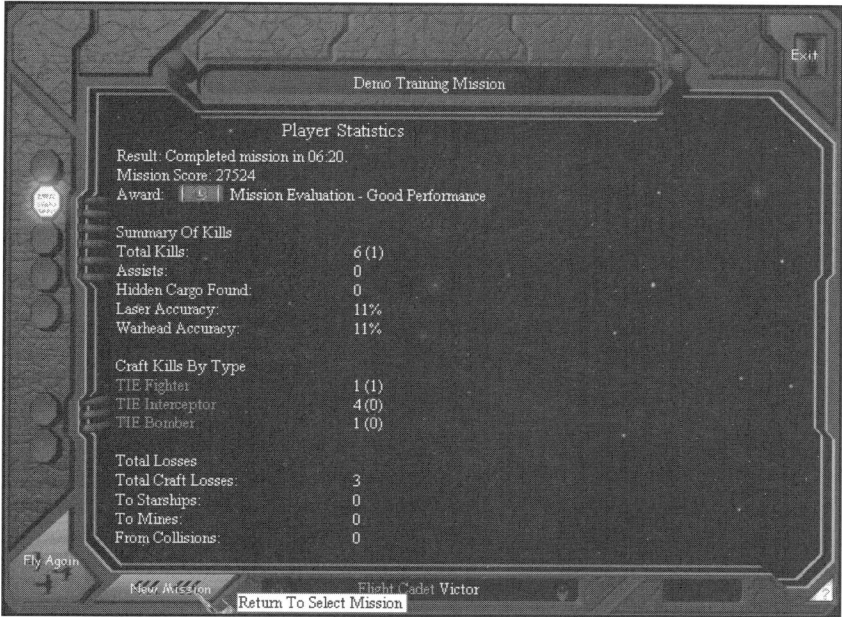

Figure 19.6: The X-Wing Alliance Demo provides a detailed performance review for each mission that can include commendations and promotions.

any shareware site on the Internet, as well as directly from Microsoft (http://www.microsoft.com). A 100% DirectX compatible sound card is required, as are a joystick, mouse and keyboard. 3D graphics accelerators are supported, but not required, and the game plays quite well on a computer with only the minimum configuration.

Visit the LucasArts home page at http://www.lucasarts.com to download this and other free demos of their popular game software.

Program Name:	X-Wing Alliance Demo Version 1.0® 1999
Program Type:	Demo
Company:	LucasArts Entertainment Company, LLC
Web Page:	http://www.lucasarts.com
Registration Fee:	None. Contact LucasArts or your software retailer for pricing on the full version of this program.

General Evaluation: X-Wing Alliance Demo Version 1.0				
	Excellent	*Good*	*Average*	*Poor*
Level of Challenge		***		
Ability to Maintain Interest		***		
Graphics and Sound		***		
Ease of Learning		***		
Documentation		***		
Overall Rating		***		

VR Sports Powerboat Racing Demo®

This devilishly difficult to master speed boat racing simulation program demo pits a human player against five computer-generated racing opponents in a fast-paced two-lap race. The game allows a player to select one of three boats with which to race and provides a single course set in New York Harbor. (The commercial version of the game provides a wide variety of race courses and type of races unavailable in this interactive trial version of the program.) Realistic sounds and graphics effects that include traffic on bridges, water skiers next to the race course and low-flying planes and helicopters during game play, add a touch of realism.

Game controls are simple: cursor control keys steer the boat and control the throttle. But controlling the high-speed boat around the race course is no easy task; were it not for the fact that crashing the boat against walls, other ships and competing racers is not possible (to say nothing of running over spectators in the water too close to the race course) I would not have been able to finish the two laps in my first ten attempts. Flipping the boat over during full-throttle jumps during the race seems to be the only way of being disqualified from finishing, a fact that did not prevent me from finishing dead last in my first half dozen attempts.

System requirements for this game are modest: Pentium 120 MHz or greater (P133 recommended) with 16mb RAM and 130MB free space on hard drive; Windows 95/98; Direct X 5.0 or later; Direct X compatible sound card and video card with 1 MB video memory; 100% windows 95 compatible keyboard, mouse and joystick or steering wheel (optional). The game supports 3D accelerator cards, but does not require them for smooth operation.

Chapter 19 : Arcade-Style Games

Figure 19.7: Aside from its forgiving nature when it comes to crashes, this game brings a high degree of realism to the playing environment that includes solid graphics and sound support. A map of the race course showing the player's current position and any nearby competitors can be superimposed on the lower left hand corner of the screen to help you navigate. Even so, it isn't difficult to stray off course. The upper portion of the screen shows vital game stats, including the player's current place in the upper left hand corner of the screen, the number of laps completed (center) and the elapsed time (right).

Program Name:	VR Sports Powerboat Racing Demo® 1997
Program Type:	Demo
Company:	Interplay Productions, Ltd.
Address:	16815 Von Karman
	Irvine, CA 92606
Web Pages:	http://www.interplay.com
	http://www.eastpoint@netmatters.co.uk
E-Mail:	Europe@Interplay.com
Registration Fee:	None. Contact Interplay Productions or your software retailer for current pricing on the full version of this program.

General Evaluation: VR Sports Powerboat Racing Demo				
	Excellent	*Good*	*Average*	*Poor*
Level of Challenge	***			
Ability to Maintain Interest		***		
Graphics and Sound	***			
Ease of Learning	***			
Documentation			***	
Overall Rating	***			

Elite Air Hockey®

Elite Air Hockey plays just like the traditional penny arcade favorite. Game play provides a remarkably realistic implementation of this classic arcade table game, even without the customizable features available only in the full game that permit customizing such variables as puck density and air pressure.

The computer opponent in this demo version is easy to trounce, since the game is limited to a single-player, beginner mode played in a stadium setting. (The commercial version of the game has five levels of difficulty and allows for multi-player games, including Internet play.) Nonetheless, users will appreciate the realism offered by this beautifully rendered game. Even the background crowd noise and music are both pleasant and well rendered; the crowd is clearly rooting for the home team, moderately cheering every point won, and decorously remaining silent upon points lost. Purposely scoring several goals into my own net produced not a whisper of disappointment from the virtual crowd; this welcomed civility was a refreshing change from the rude noises one would expect in a real game under similar circumstances, and one real sports fans would do well to emulate.

Program Name:	Elite Air Hockey® 1999
Program Type:	Demo
Company:	Perpetual Motion Enterprises, Inc.
Address:	202 New Edition Court
	Cary, NC 27513
Web Page:	http://www.pmenterprises.com
Registration Fee:	None. Contact Perpetual Motion Enterprises or your software retailer for current pricing on the full version of this program.

Chapter 19 : Arcade-Style Games 159

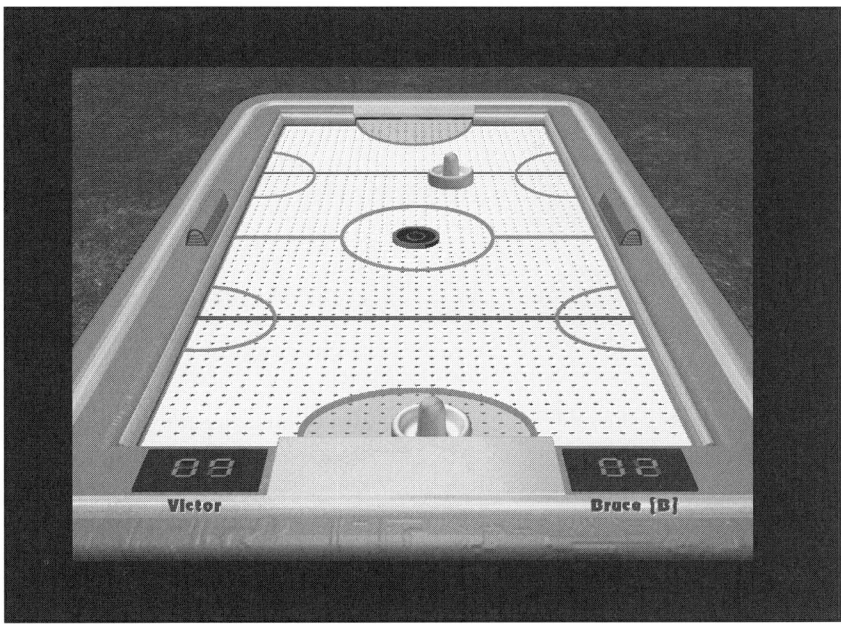

Figure 19.8: *Elite Air Hockey perfectly recreates the classic table game with a high level of realism, while adding aesthetically pleasing background sounds and music. You can almost feel the gentle rush of the air brushing against your hand as you play this well implemented game.*

General Evaluation: Elite Air Hockey® 1999

	Excellent	Good	Average	Poor
Level of Challenge		***		
Ability to Maintain Interest		***		
Graphics and Sound	***			
Ease of Learning	***			
Documentation			***	
Overall Rating			***	

Chapter 20
GAMES OF STRATEGY

From the traditional chess and checkers board games dating back to the eighth century A.D. to the classic games such as Tic Tac Toe and Battleship, games of strategy have long been favored by players of all ages. The advent of the computer has little changed these games, save for the opportunity to engage in these favorite pastimes even when a human opponent is unavailable. Unlike their flashier modern counterparts that often promote excitement and reward quick reflexes, these quieter, gentler games promote and reward critical thinking and problem solving skills. Given that most of the games in this chapter can be played in a small window while viewing other programs that run in the background, they provide an ideal way of passing the time and exercising one's brain while waiting for long files to download or graphics-rich web pages to be accessed.

E.G. Chess® Version 1.0.3

E.G. Chess represents a solid Windows 95/98 implementation the classic game. The program allows two human players to play each other by using the computer-generated 3D game board, and permits a player to play against himself. Network play is also supported, as is play against the computer in any of four difficulty levels.

The novice player will appreciate the program's help file which incorporates a graphics-enhanced tutorial on the game of chess that covers the fundamental rules of the game and the movement of individual chess pieces. Background music and sounds are available and can be switched on or off at the player's option. A particularly nice feature of the game is

Chapter 20 : Games of Strategy

Figure 20.1: *E.G. Chess offers a good combination of play options with a solid chess engine program that offers quick, challenging play at any of four available difficulty levels. The board can be rotated left or right as well as up and down to give players an optimum view of the game board during play.*

the ability to rotate the chess board in any direction clockwise, counter clockwise and with respect to the player's overhead perspective of the board via the mouse or keyboard. This allows a player to view the board from any angle at any time during game play, and to shift the perspective from directly over the board (rendering play two dimensional) to any side.

The chess engine will give most players a very challenging game with a minimum of delay, even on slower systems.

Program Name:	E.G. Chess Version 1.0.3® 1999
Program Type:	Shareware
Company:	Earth Gaming
Address:	#12, 1395 West 13 Ave
	Vancouver, BC, Canada
	Postal Code V6H 1N7

| | Excellent | Good | Average | Poor |

Web Page: http://www.nucleus.com/~npl/
E-mail: npl@nucleus.com
Registration Fee: $5. On-line credit card registration is supported at http://www.nucleus.com/~npl/chess/chess.html.

General Evaluation: E.G. Chess Version 1.0.3

	Excellent	Good	Average	Poor
Level of Challenge		***		
Ability to Maintain Interest		***		
Graphics and Sound		***		
Ease of Learning		***		
Documentation		***		
Overall Rating		***		

Plus700® Version 6.06

Plus700 is an incredibly powerful and flexible checkers program that can be customized to serve as a training tool for a beginner or serve as a powerful opponent to even the best of players.

The program's documentation claims that Plus700 is a "self teaching" program that becomes more challenging the more one plays with it. That is a claim I cannot substantiate since it resoundingly beat me every game I played at the fourth of ten competitive levels. Despite its power, the program offers crisp play at most levels, even on low-end Pentium systems. (According to its documentation, moves on a Pentium 100 range from 1 second at level 3 to 5–6 seconds on level 4, 35–30 seconds on level 5 and 150–200 seconds on level 6. Beyond level 6, however, game play slows down to a painful crawl, even on relatively fast systems. On my Compaq Armada 1750 (Pentium II 350), the first computer move on level 6 took 46 seconds. At level 8, the time was more than 5 minutes, and at level 10, the computer had not moved after a full 40 minutes. The game allows the setting of difficulty levels from 1 through 40. At levels minus one, zero and one, I could more than hold my own against the computer. But at level four, the computer trounced me every time. (I am better at chess than checkers, but I trust even a good player would find anything above level four a good challenge.)

In addition to a wide range of difficulty settings, the game allows a player to set up a board any way he or she chooses, adding or deleting

Chapter 20 : Games of Strategy

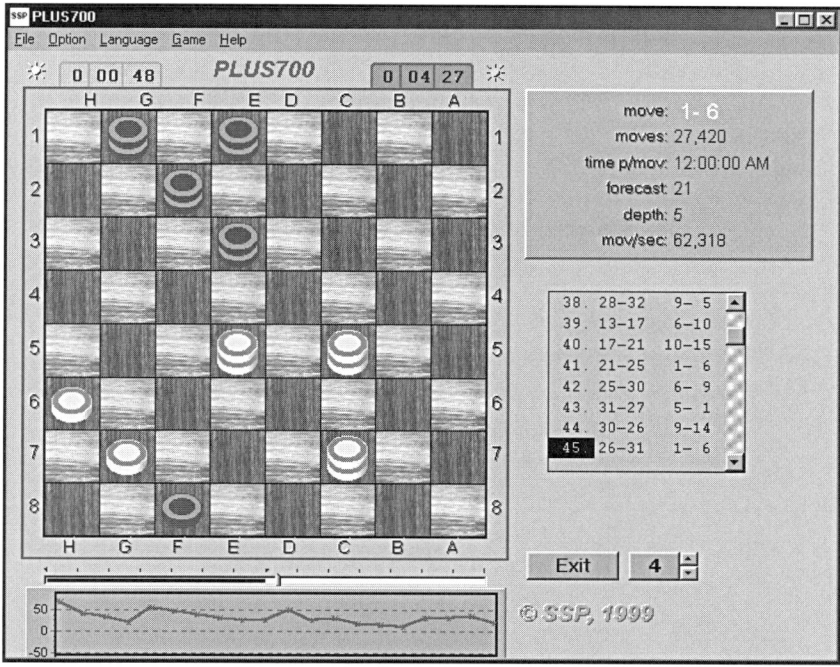

Figure 20.2: Plus700 is a powerful checkers program for Windows 95/98 that will challenge players of every level. The program's documentation is quite thin and suffers from an imperfect translation from the Russian original, and selecting the Help menu merely pops up a brief "About" notice. Nonetheless, this is a very minor shortcoming given the intuitive nature of the program.

pieces at will in order to practice play variations or to handicap him/herself or the computer opponent. Saving and retrieving games in progress is also supported in the shareware version, a must for games played at the higher levels given the time they will require for completion. The game also supports Russian or English language play. (English language documentation is a bit rough, but certainly understandable.)

If you are a checkers player, you will find little to dislike in this remarkable implementation of the game. If you don't already like or play the game, this program can will likely provide you with a new appreciation and respect for the game.

Program Name: Plus700® Version 6.06 1985–1999
Program Type: Shareware

Programmer / Copyright Owner:	Serge Startsev
Web Page:	http://www.geocities.com/TimesSquare/1708
E-mail:	sergst@hotmail.com
Registration Fee:	$21

General Evaluation: Plus700 Version 6.06

	Excellent	*Good*	*Average*	*Poor*
Level of Challenge	***			
Ability to Maintain Interest	***			
Graphics and Sound	***			
Ease of Learning	***			
Documentation			***	
Overall Rating	***			

Bloch Reversi® Version 3.0.3

The game of Reversi is deceptively simple to learn, yet difficult to master. Players begin with two black or white pieces in the center of a checkered board. Players then take turns placing pieces on the board in such a way as to trap the opponent's game pieces vertically, horizontally or diagonally between two of the player's game pieces. When this happens, the opponent's pieces flip over and change color, becoming the player's pieces. Pieces can only be placed in squares that result in the opponent's pieces being "trapped" between the moving player's own black or white colored game pieces. A player who cannot trap the opponent's pieces in a given move must pass and allow the opposing player to move. Whoever controls the most game pieces at the end of the game wins.

Bloch Reversi can be played by two human opponents, or by a human opponent against the computer. Even in the lowest of three available difficulty levels, the computer is a formidable opponent. The on-line help system gives clear, brief illustrated instructions that will have anyone playing the game within minutes. The computer can even be called upon to offer hints as to the best move at any time at the press of a mouse button. Moves can also be taken back after they are made. At the conclusion of each game, a graphic representation of each player's performance tracking each game move automatically pops up, giving players a snapshot overview of their performance during the game. A game replay option is available that quickly and smoothly shows every move of the last game.

Chapter 20 : Games of Strategy

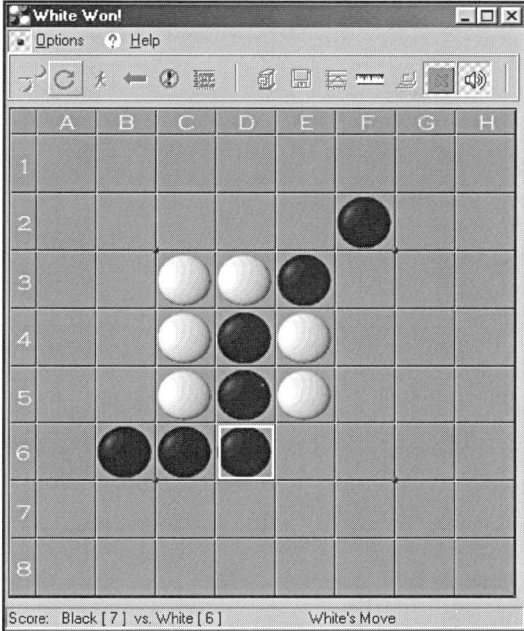

Figure 20.3: Bloch Reversi *offers remarkably challenging game play even in the lowest of its three difficulty levels. The game is easy to learn but difficult to master and will give your critical thinking skills a good workout.*

Finally, the game board window can be resized into one of three preset sizes. In the smallest of these, the game can be played in a window that takes up approximately 25% of the computer's desktop, giving an ample view of other programs running in the background.

Block Reversi is another excellent computer rendition of a game of strategy that can keep you entertained for hours, whether you play against the computer or a friend.

Program Name:	Bloch Reversi® Version 3.0.3 1999
Program Type:	Shareware
Programmer / Copyright Owner:	John Bloch
Address:	1514 Stallings Rd. Durham, NC 27703
Web Page:	http://www.blochweb.com
Registration Fee:	$8

Unit V : Games

General Evaluation: Bloch Reversi Version 3.0.3				
	Excellent	Good	Average	Poor
Level of Challenge		***		
Ability to Maintain Interest		***		
Graphics and Sound		***		
Ease of Learning		***		
Documentation		***		
Overall Rating		***		

Kyodai® Version 2.88

Kyodai is computerized version of the classic solitaire game Mah Jongg. The object of the game is to successfully remove all of the tiles from the play area as quickly as possible. Tiles are removed by clicking on matching pairs, two by two, but a tile may be removed only if no other tile touches either its left or right border.

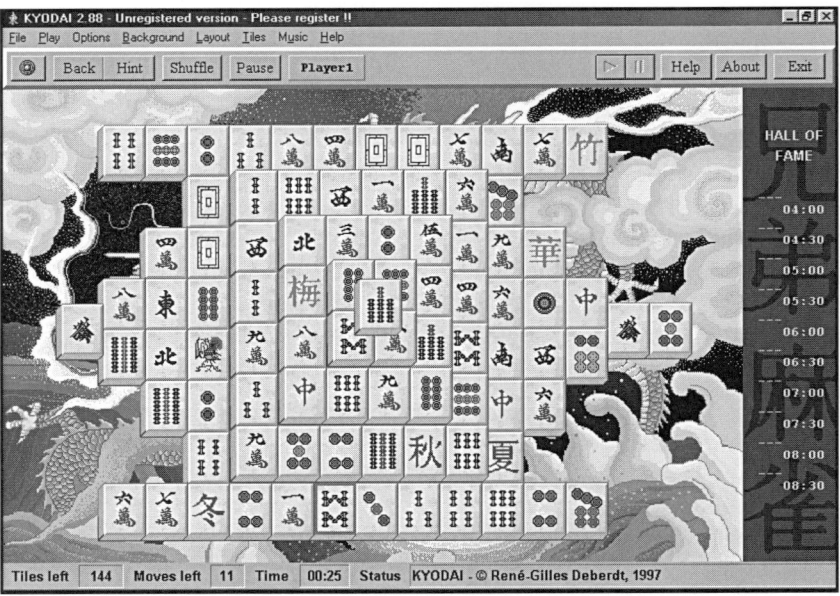

Figure 20.4: Kyodai is an electronic version of the classic solitaire game Mah Jongg featuring beautiful graphics and sound along with a highly customizable game environment.

The game offers five different layouts, each providing a different level of difficulty. Sound effects and four beautiful background musical schemes are available but can be switched off, and the background and colors of the tiles can be customized to suit the player's taste. The player is given a great deal of control over game play that includes the ability to pause the game, take back moves, reshuffle tiles and have the computer suggest available valid moves.

This shareware game will pop up a nagging reminder to register the program several times during game play. Normally this would disqualify the game from consideration for inclusion in this book. The relatively unobtrusive reminders seemed reasonable, however, given that the shareware version of the game has no expiration date, is fully functional, and its registration fee is relatively modest.

Program Name:	Kiodai® Version 2.88 1997
Program Type:	Shareware
Programmer / Copyright Owner:	Rene-Gilles Deberdt
Address:	80 rue Gauthier
	62400 Bethune
	France
Web Page:	http://www.namida.com/mahjongg.en.html
Registration Fee:	$15 in cash (no checks) You can also register on-line for $16 at http://kyodai.home.ml.org

General Evaluation: Kiodai Version 2.88

	Excellent	Good	Average	Poor
Level of Challenge		***		
Ability to Maintain Interest	***			
Graphics and Sound	***			
Ease of Learning	***			
Documentation			***	
Overall Rating	***			

Mind's Tic Tac Toe® Version 1.0

Tic Tac Toe may not be the most challenging of games, given that the natural conclusion to any game by two thoughtful players ought be a draw. Nevertheless, it is a game that nearly all of us learned and played

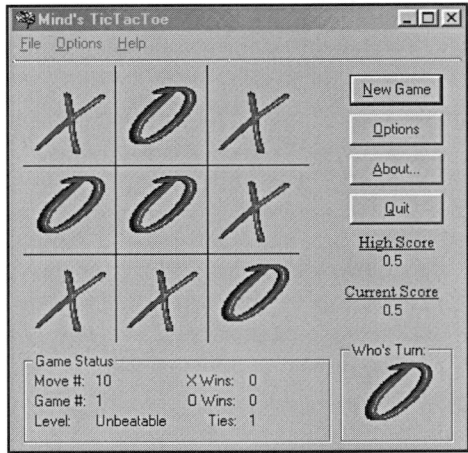

Figure 20.5: *Mind's Tic Tac Toe updates an old standard with nice graphics, sounds and the option of playing against a human or computer opponent.*

as children, and it certainly represents a challenge to younger players, as well as a good introduction to games of strategy.

This version of the game features well implemented graphics and sounds that will be particularly welcomed by younger players. Game play can be set to one of four levels ranging from "easy" to "unbeatable" that can provide increasing challenge to new players as they learn the basic strategy of the game, while boosting their confidence at being able to beat the computer at increasing levels of difficulty. At the highest setting, a draw is the natural conclusion of every game, though playing quickly and thoughtlessly will certainly result in defeat for children or adults alike. The game supports play between two opponents or between one player and the computer. A high score list is also maintained.

Overall, this is the nicest implementation of the game I have seen to date, and it is free.

Program Name:	Mind's Tic Tac Toe® Version 1.0 1997
Program Type:	Freeware
Company:	Mind Products
Programmer / Copyright Owner:	Donovan Parks
E-Mail:	donopark@awinc.co
Web Page:	http://www.geocities.com/area51/8315/mpindex.htm
Registration Fee:	None.

Chapter 20 : Games of Strategy 169

General Evaluation: Mind's Tic Tac Toe Version 1.0

	Excellent	Good	Average	Poor
Level of Challenge		***		
Ability to Maintain Interest		***		
Graphics and Sound	***			
Ease of Learning	***			
Documentation			***	
Overall Rating		***		

Connect It® Version 1.0

In this computerized version of a popular children's game, the object is to drop chips into one of seven slots so that four chips of the same color are aligned either vertically, horizontally or diagonally. The concept is simple enough to be grasped by young children, but the strategy required

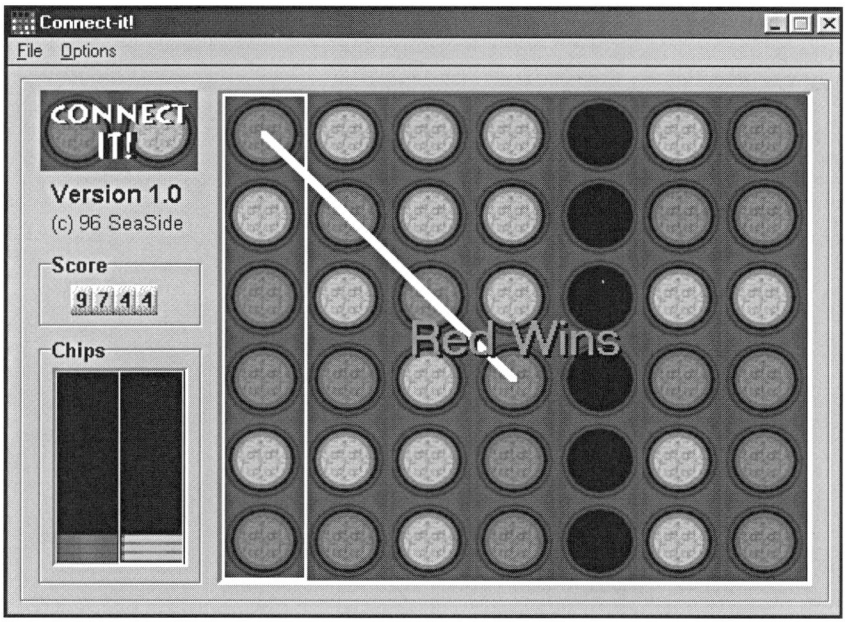

Figure 20.6: *In Connect It, a player takes turns with the computer opponent dropping game pieces down one of seven columns. The first player to get four game pieces in a row horizontally, vertically or diagonally wins.*

to beat the computer at the standard setting will provide a good challenge to adult players as well. The game allows for play at two levels of difficulty: standard and easy. Game play is swift in both levels. The shareware version of the game allows only for play against the computer; upon registration, however, the game will allow play between two human opponents. High score tables are maintained.

The game does not provide a help file or any documentation, but the intuitive interface and menu system are self-explanatory, and any player unfamiliar with the rules of game play would quickly learn them by playing one or two games against the computer.

Program Name:	Connect It® Version 1.0 1996
Program Type:	Shareware (30 day free trial. Software must be registered or deleted after the trial period by the user.)
Company:	SeaSide Studios
Address:	L. Safranyik
	141 Durrance Rd.
	Victoria, B.C, Canada,
	V8X 4M6
Web Page:	HTTP://www.islandnet.com
Support E-mail:	isafrany@uvic.ca
Registration Fee:	$6

General Evaluation: Connect It Version 1.0

	Excellent	Good	Average	Poor
Level of Challenge		***		
Ability to Maintain Interest		***		
Graphics and Sound		***		
Ease of Learning	***			
Documentation				***
Overall Rating		***		

Ultra Logic® Version 2.0

Ultra Logic is a computerized version of the classic Master Mind game. As is true of most enduring games, its rules are simple, yet mastering this challenging game requires concentration, deductive reasoning and solid analytical skills.

Chapter 20 : Games of Strategy

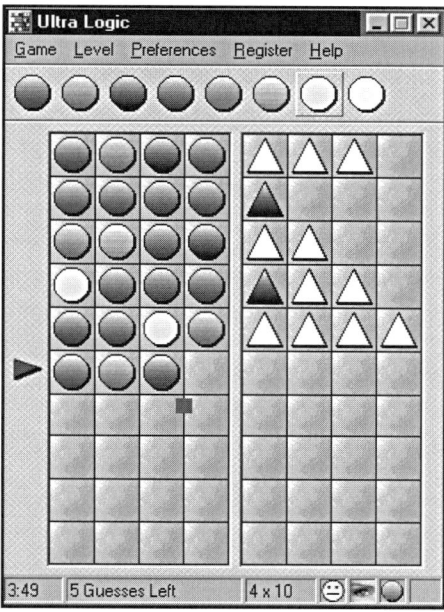

Figure 20.7: Even in Beginner Mode, Ultra Logic provides an intellectual challenge. In the game in progress shown here, the first guess (blue, green, black, purple) results in three white triangles as feedback from the computer. This means three of the four color guesses were accurate, but not their sequence of selection. Through deductive reasoning, the fifth guess results in uncovering the correct colors of the combination (blue, purple, aqua, green) not its sequence. The final guess on row six, in the process of being completed here, will result in the right combination: purple, green, blue, aqua. Once the last color is entered, four black triangles will be displayed and the winning combination acknowledged.

The game presents the player with the task of deducing a randomly generated key made up of colored balls in a specific sequence. A player is given ten guesses to determine the colors and the sequence of a set of colored balls selected by the computer. The number of balls varies depending on the difficulty level selected; the shareware game allows from four to six colored ball combinations out of eight possible ball colors for the beginner, intermediate and advanced levels, respectively. Since a player is limited to ten guesses in the beginner and advanced levels, and nine guesses in the intermediate level, the difficulty level rises accordingly (See Figure 20.7 for a sample easy game involving a four ball combination.) The registered version of the game allows even greater flexibility in by permitting an expert and custom grid option.

In order to complete each move, a player selects each ball by double clicking on it and dragging it to the desired slot. The computer giver feedback after each guess or four to six balls is made by giving one of three responses: no response, a white triangle or a black triangle. No response means none of the colors guessed are a part of the combination. A white diamond appears for each color selected correctly, but signifies the color was not chosen in the proper sequence. A black triangle signifies that a ball with the proper color and proper sequence appears in the player's current guess. Thus, if the combination chosen by the computer is, say, red, green, blue, yellow and a player guesses black, purple, red, gray, the computer would respond with a single white triangle, meaning one of the colors guesses was correct (red), but does not appear in the correct order. A guess of red, grey, purple, black under the same facts would produce a black triangle, meaning only one of the colors selected appears in the code and it is in the proper sequence (which color, of course, must be deduced by the player through additional guesses.)

Ultra Logic incorporates a useful tutorial and help system and provides sound effects and music that can be switched on or off to suit the user's preference.

Program Name:	Ultra Logic® Version 2.0 1996, 1997
Program Type:	Shareware (21 day free trial. Software must be registered or deleted after the trial period by the user.)
Programmer / Copyright Owner:	Vitaly Livshits
Address:	Vitaly Livshits 605 Finch Ave. West, Apt 517 North York, Ontario M2R 1P1 Canada
E-mail:	ultralogic@poboxes.com
Registration Fee:	$20

General Evaluation: Ultra Logic Version 2.0

	Excellent	*Good*	*Average*	*Poor*
Level of Challenge	***			
Ability to Maintain Interest	***			
Graphics and Sound			***	
Ease of Learning	***			
Documentation	***			
Overall Rating	***			

Submarine 2®

Submarine 2 is based on the traditional game of Battleship. In this version of the game, a player is pitted against the computer in a battle to be the first to sink all of the ships in the other player's fleet.

As in the classic game it emulates, each side places a fleet of ten ships on a 10 by 10 square grid. Each fleet contains ships of varying sizes from one to four squares. A player can manually place his or her fleet by clicking on individual grid squares until the whole fleet is strategically deployed in accordance with the player's wishes, or the computer can randomly place

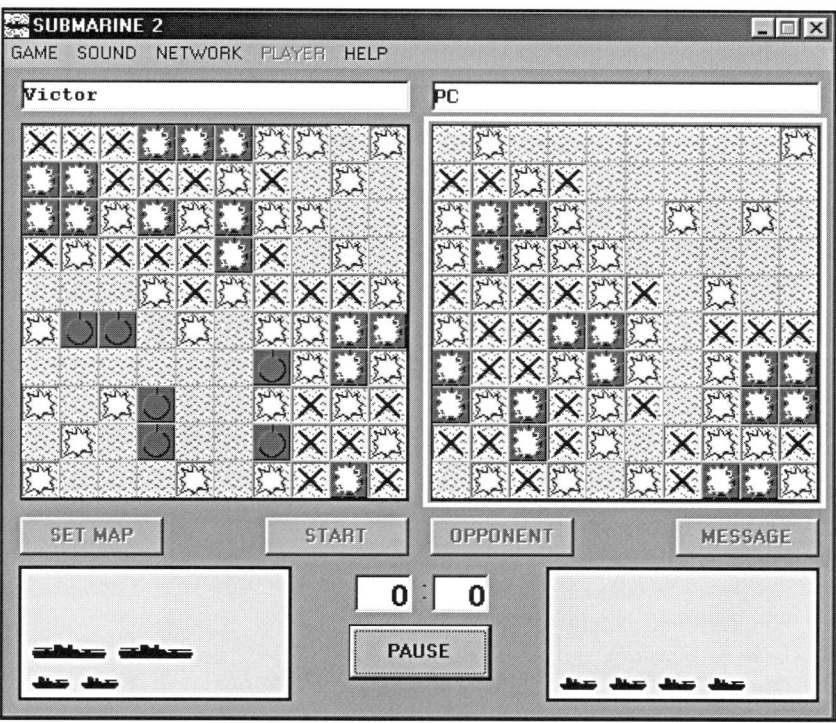

Figure 20.8: *The player's ship deployments are shown on the left side of the screen, while the computer's on the right remain hidden until a successful hit is scored. After scoring a hit, the grid square representing the portion of the ship hit is shown ablaze, while misses are shown in lighter outlines. The computer and human player alternate taking shots at one another's fleets, and an extra shot can be taken any time a hit is scored. Once all squares in a multi-square ship are hit, the ship is outlined with X marks around it and its profile is removed from the bottom portion of the screen that shows the remaining ships in the fleet.*

the entire fleet on the player's grid by pressing the Set Map button; if the latter option is selected, the placement of the fleet varies every time the on screen button is pressed, allowing a player to cycle through random fleet placements until a desired one is found. Once the fleet is deployed, play begins with the human player and the computer taking turns firing torpedoes at one another's ships, accompanied by appropriate sound affects.

Winning the game requires both luck and strategy: luck in guessing the location of the enemy's ships, and strategy both in the placement of the player's fleet and in selecting a firing pattern likely to hit the enemy ships in the fewest attempts possible.

Submarine 2 supports play against the computer and network play against other human opponents.

Program Name: Submarine 2® 1999
Program Type: Shareware (30 day free trial. Software expires after the trial period.)
Programmer / Copyright Owner: Krešimir Vajn
Address: Sv. Roka 54
31000 Osijek
Croatia
E-mail: kvajn@os.tel.hr
Registration Fee: $5

General Evaluation: Submarine 2

	Excellent	*Good*	*Average*	*Poor*
Level of Challenge		***		
Ability to Maintain Interest		***		
Graphics and Sound		***		
Ease of Learning	***			
Documentation		***		
Overall Rating		***		

CHAPTER 21
CARD GAMES

Most Windows 95/98 users are familiar with the Microsoft Solitaire, Hearts and FreeCell solitaire games that are bundled with the operating system. Users who like these games will be pleased by the wide range of other card games available as free or try-before-you-buy programs. In this chapter, we'll examine a cross section of the titles available in this genre of entertainment software.

Canasta for Windows 95/98/NT® Version 4.14

If you play or would like to learn to play the game of Canasta, this program will be a welcomed addition to your software library.

The program permits two player games with the computer as an opponent or with another player over a network. Good graphics and sound along with a host of customizable features are available, along with three difficulty levels when playing against the computer. The shareware version of this game is fully functional, with one exception: each game is limited to 25 different hands. Upon registration, this limitation is lifted.

Canasta for Windows 95/98/NT incorporates a useful help system that can teach the rudimentary rules of the game very quickly. Although I am familiar with numerous card games, I seldom play card games and have never played Canasta, yet I could play the game within minutes by consulting the help system and beat the computer in my first attempt at the beginner level.

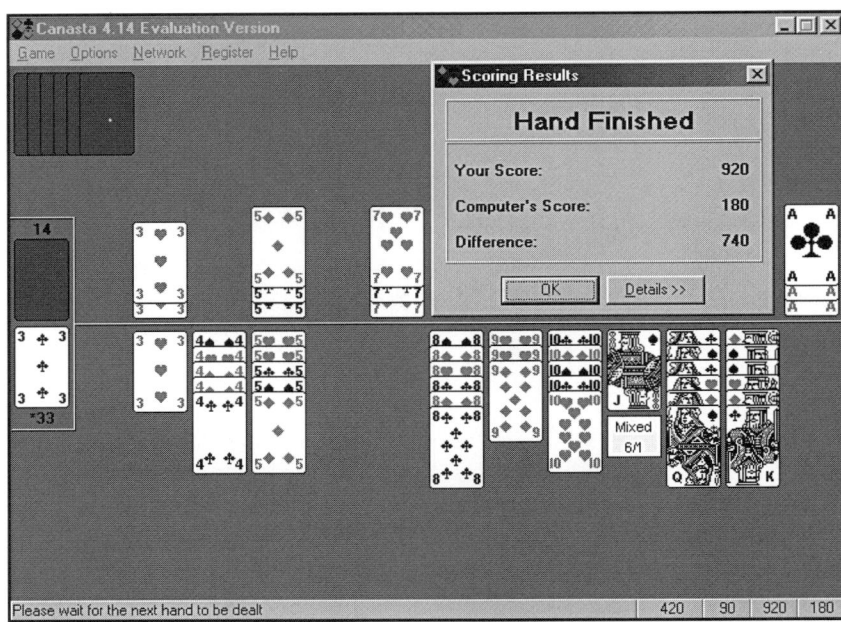

Figure 21.1: *A host of customizable features accompanied by a good help system and three levels of computer play make Canasta for Windows 95/98/NT an interesting and challenging game.*

Program Name:	Canasta for Windows 95/98/NT® Version 4.14 1993-1999
Program Type:	Shareware (Play limited to 25 hands in any game.)
Programmer/ Copyright Owner:	Mark-Jan Harte
Address:	Cort v.d. Lindenlaan 84 1412 CB Naarden The Netherlands
Web Page:	http://www.canasta.net
E-mail:	masta@zap.a2000.nl
Registration Fee:	$19.95 (If paying by check, funds must be drawn on a U.S. bank.)

General Evaluation: Canasta for Windows 95/98/NT

	Excellent	*Good*	*Average*	*Poor*
Level of Challenge	***			
Ability to Maintain Interest	***			

	Excellent	Good	Average	Poor
Graphics and Sound	***			
Ease of Learning	***			
Documentation	***			
Overall Rating	***			

Free Solitaire® Version 1.02

If you like playing the solitaire games bundled with Windows 95/98, you will love this well integrated freeware package of six different card games. Good graphics, documentation and playing instructions for each game make this a terrific package that every fan of solitaire card games will like.

Forty Thieves, Free Cell, Klondike, Pyramid, Sea Haven Towers and Spider are the solitaire games included in this package. (See Figures 21.2–21.9 for illustrations of each game.) The user may select from three different deck designs and may also choose the background color. Right clicking on any of the six games pops up a help window that includes the rules for playing the game, instructions for playing the game, game objectives and strategies, along with the odds of winning a hand.

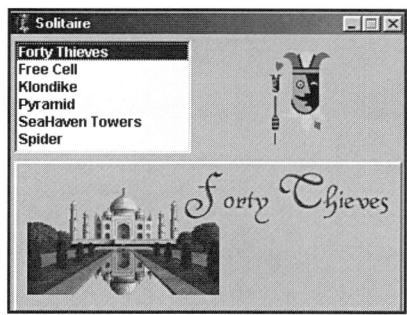

Figure 21.2: Free Solitaire's opening window allows a user to select from six available solitaire card games. Double clicking on a game brings up a scalable window. If you are not familiar with a given game, a help window can be accessed once the game is loaded by right-clicking anywhere on the game screen. Available help for every game is brief, direct, clear and informative. (For a sample help screen, use Figure 21.3.)

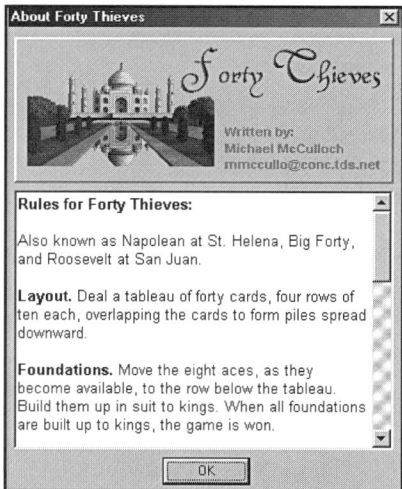

Figure 21.3: Help window for Forty Thieves.

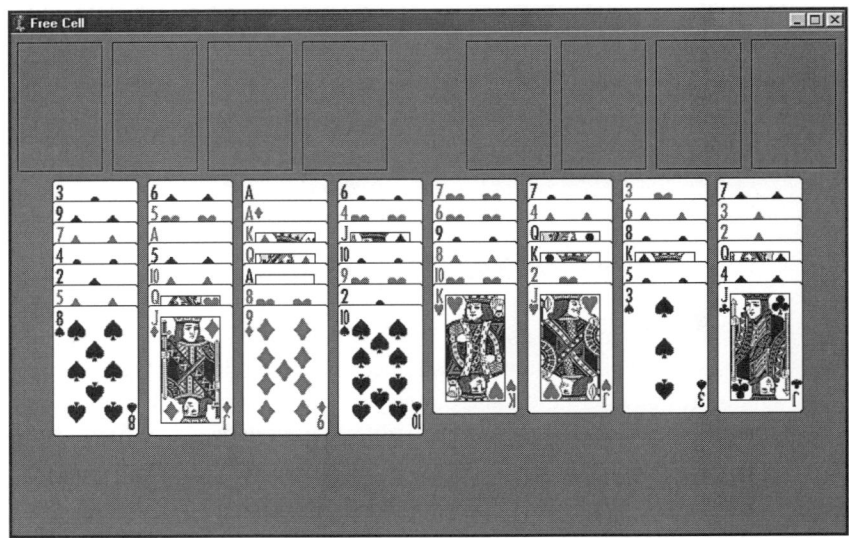

Figure 21.4: Forty Thieves

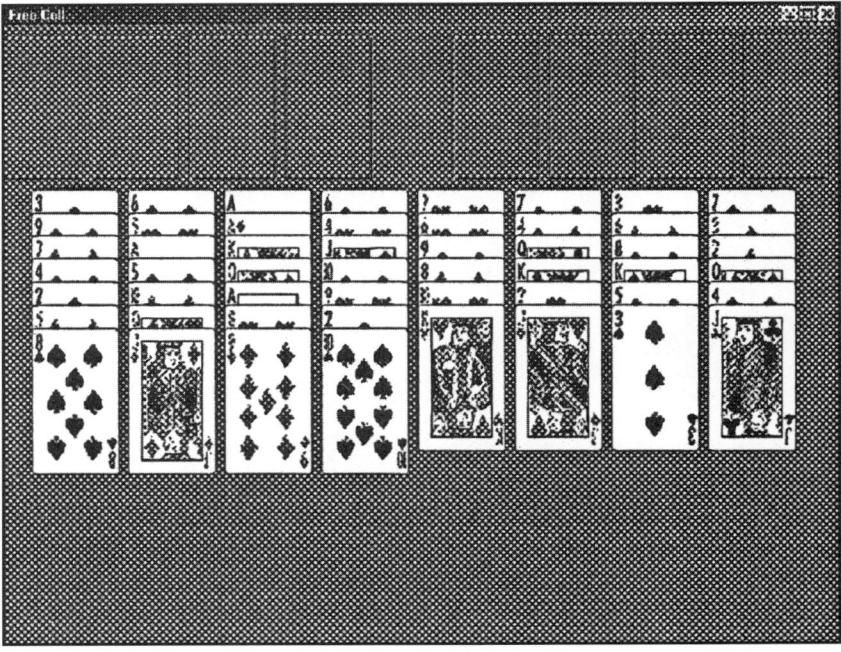

Figure 21.5: Free Cell

Chapter 21 : Card Games

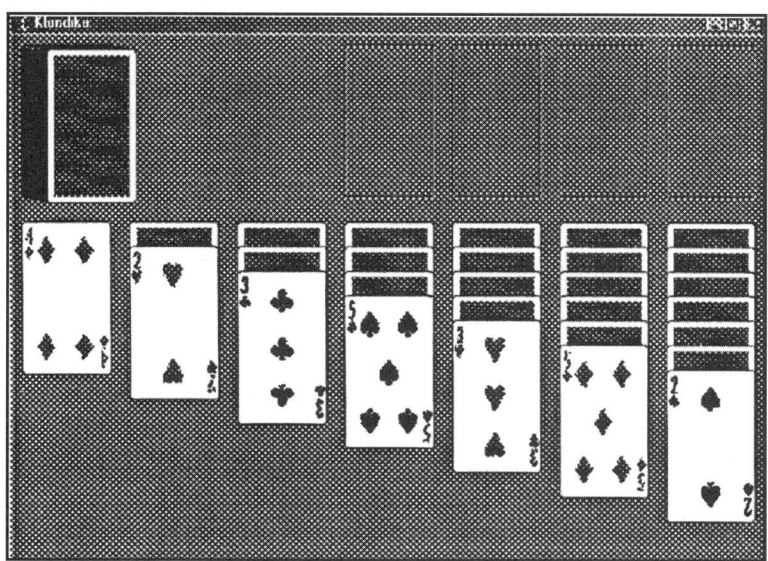

Figure 21.6: Klondike

Figure 21.7: Pyramid

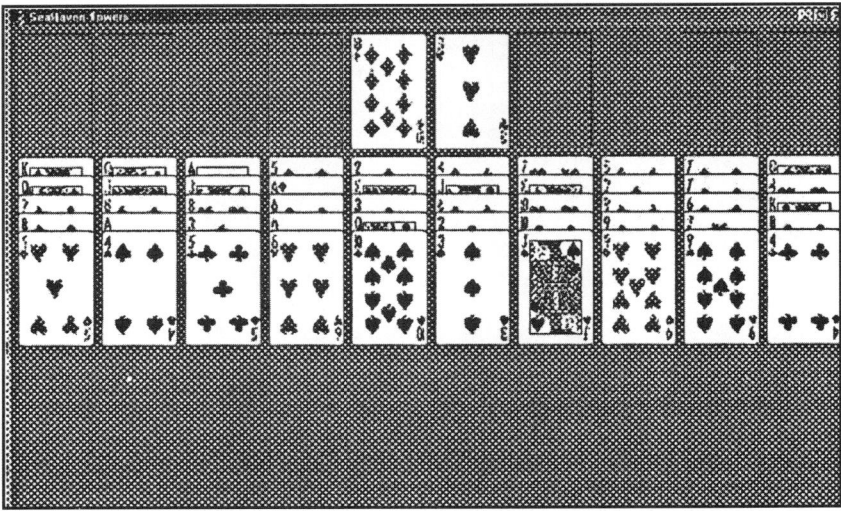

Figure 21.8: Sea Haven Towers

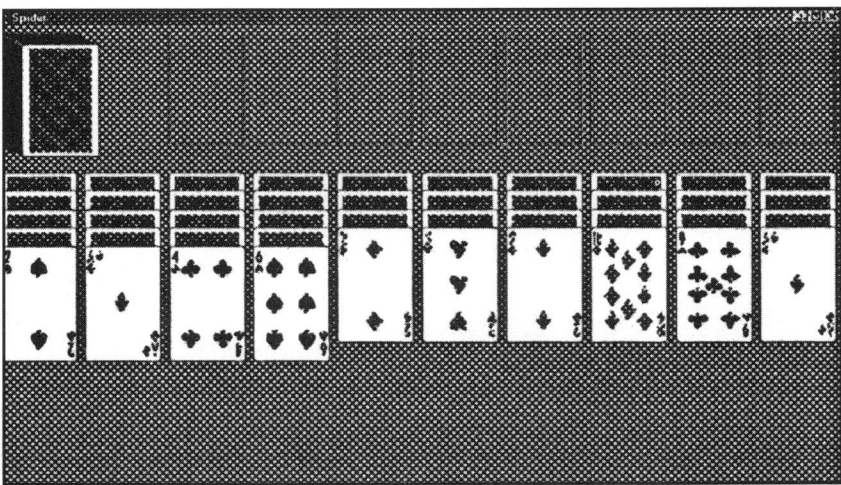

Figure 21.9: Spider

If you intend to download this software package be warned: your productivity may suffer. On the other hand, playing these games while you wait to connect to your ISP or for that graphics-intensive web page to load can certainly make the wait almost bearable, and it might even help ward against incipient catatonia. Recommended.

Program Name:	Free Solitaire® Version 1.02 1997
Program Type:	Freeware
Programmer/ Copyright Owner:	Michael McCulloch Knoxville, TN
E-mail:	mmccullo@conc.tds.net
Registration Fee:	None.

General Evaluation: Free Solitaire Version 1.02

	Excellent	*Good*	*Average*	*Poor*
Level of Challenge		***		
Ability to Maintain Interest		***		
Graphics and Sound			***	
Ease of Learning		***		
Documentation		***		
Overall Rating		***		

JSpades® Version 1.02

If you are a Spades player, this version of the game should bring you hours of pleasure in play against three computer opponents. If you are unfamiliar with the game, however, you will need to learn it prior to installing the software, since this otherwise excellent game will not give you assistance with the rules of the game.

JSpades offers a high level of customization, allowing the player to select four playing speeds, seven different deck designs and even four colors and textures for the play surface. The winning score is also user-selectable at either 250 or 500 points. No sound effects are available, as is typical of most card games, but the quality of the graphics is quite good. Best of all, this game is free.

Program Name:	JSpades® 1.02 1997
Program Type:	Freeware
Company:	J. Ollman & Associates
Address:	P.O. Box 540004 North Salt Lake, UT 84054-0004
Web Page:	http://pobox.com/~j.ollman
E-mail:	j.ollman@pobox.com
Registration Fee:	None.

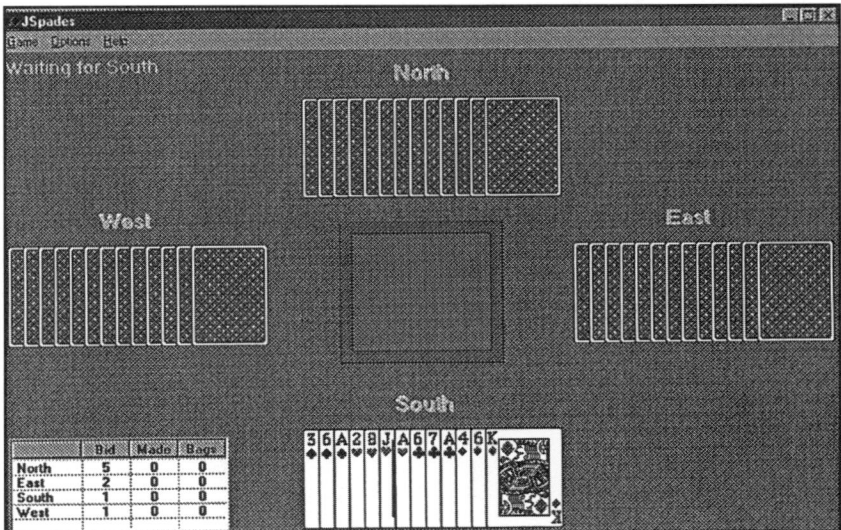

Figure 21.10: *JSpades Version 1.02 offers a highly customizable implementation of the game of Spades.*

General Evaluation: JSpades Version 1.02				
	Excellent	*Good*	*Average*	*Poor*
Level of Challenge		***		
Ability to Maintain Interest		***		
Graphics and Sound		***		
Ease of Learning			***	
Documentation			***	
Overall Rating		***		

Noisy Video Poker/Blackjack® for Windows 95 Version 4.6

Noisy Video Poker/Blackjack for Windows 95 lives up to its name, providing two separate video card games full of loud sound effects to signal winning and losing hands.

When the program is started, a player can choose between the Noisy Video Poker or Noisy Video Blackjack games. The video poker game allows the player to bet from one to five coins in each hand, and starts the player off with a 100 coin credit. After the computer deals five cards, the

Figure 21.11: Noisy Video Poker

player can choose which card or cards to keep by clicking on them, with unwanted cards discarded and new cards dealt by the computer once the "Deal" button is clicked on (See Figure 21.11). The computer pays out coins for winning hands from one coin for a pair of Jacks of better on a one coin bet up to 4,000 coins for a royal flush on a five coin bet. Registration of Noisy Video Poker brings two additional game variations to the Jacks of Better shareware option: Joker Wild and Deuces Wild.

Noisy Video Blackjack is a standard video blackjack game. The player may bet from one to five coins each hand. Upon registration, two additional features are activated: the ability to split pairs and to buy insurance against a dealer's blackjack.

Both games offer good graphics and sound effects, although the latter can become tiresome quickly and can mercifully be turned off. (The cartoon-like sounds of broken springs, crashing cars, gunfire, and farm animals to signal losing hands were amusing the first and second times they were heard, but quickly became tiresome; likewise the happier winning sounds.)

Figure 21.12: Noisy Video Blackjack

Program Name:	Noisy Video Poker/Blackjack® for Windows 95 Version 4.6 1994-1997
Program Type:	Shareware (30 day license. Users must register after the 30 day trial or uninstall the software from their systems.)
Company:	Ultimate Software, Inc.
Address:	P.O. Box 5015 Central Point, OR 97502
Web Page:	http://www.softsite.com/ulti/
E-mail:	ultisoft@mind.net
Registration Fee:	$20 each for Noisy Video Poker and Noisy Video Blackjack. $25 for both programs if registered together.

General Evaluation: Noisy Video Blackjack/Poker Version 4.6

	Excellent	Good	Average	Poor
Level of Challenge		***		

Chapter 21 : Card Games

	Excellent	Good	Average	Poor
Ability to Maintain Interest		***		
Graphics and Sound		***		
Ease of Learning	***			
Documentation	***			
Overall Rating		***		

CHAPTER 22

EDUCATIONAL GAMES

Nearly 30 years after the launch of the original IBM PC and the computer revolution that it was instrumental in bringing about, many adults are still uncomfortable with personal computers. Not so children who have never shown the combination of fear and awe of the new technology that has made it difficult for many adults to embrace the PC. In this chapter, we will examine some educational programs that capitalize on children's natural affinity for computers and games to turn the family PC into an effective teaching tool.

ABC Treehouse®

ABC Treehouse is an educational program aimed at younger children that teaches them to use the computer as they explore the contents of a virtual treehouse. Children can click on different items in the treehouse that respond in a variety of ways. A light goes on and off as a cursor touches it. Clicking on an apple, basketball and chair bring up a narrator's voice ("A is for Apple, B is for Ball, C is for Chair") and animated graphics. A magic trick is activated by clicking on a rabbit and tophat, while clicking on a book brings up a brief illustrated version of the classic "The Tortoise and the Hare" fable (minus Aesop's moral to the tale).

Good illustrations and human narration make this an engaging and entertaining game that can teach children how to use a PC while reinforcing basic reading skills. This demo version of the program is limited to the contents of the treehouse, but the full version brings two additional

Chapter 22 : Educational Games

Figure 22.1: *ABC Treehouse provides a variety of activities to young children accessible by clicking on items in the screen. Clicking on the hat icon, for example, will pop up the magic trick shown in Figure 22.2.*

Figure 22.2: *Activities such as this magic trick will make children comfortable with using the computer as a learning tool.*

Figure 22.3: *Clicking on the book icon in the program's opening screen brings a brief version of Aesop's "The Tortoise and the Hare" to life with catchy dialogue that is spoken as it is shown in cartoon balloon format so that children can read along.*

locations that children can visit by clicking on the treehouse window (Bugland and Word River).

Even so, there are enough activities here to keep a child interested in hours of productive game play. The program will run on a 486-50 or better system with 8 MB of RAM and Windows 95/98.

Program Name: ABC Treehouse® 1999
Program Type: Demo
Company: Spiral Enterprises 1, LLC
Address: 7367 Wiser LaneLynden, WA 98264
Web Page: http://www.bitstudio.com/abcorder.htm
Registration Fee: $24.95 + $3 shipping for the full version of the program.

General Evaluation: ABC Treehouse

	Excellent	Good	Average	Poor
Level of Challenge		***		
Ability to Maintain Interest		***		
Graphics and Sound	***			
Ease of Learning	***			
Documentation			***	
Overall Rating			***	

Astro Mania® Version 1.5

Astro Mania is an exceptional learning game for players of all ages that can both educate and test your knowledge of astronomy.

The program supports both a learning mode and a game mode. The learning mode provides cogent, understandable information about astronomy via brief illustrated essays that make learning about a challenging subject exciting and understandable. The game level supports seven difficulty levels and provides four different ways to play: associating the name to the picture, matching the name to a clue, associating the clue to a picture, and matching a clue to another clue. An IQ Test mode is also available, allowing you to measure your understanding of astronomy before and after engaging in the learning activities offered by this program.

This is one of the finest programs of its type I have seen both in its content and in the breath of information it provides. Unlike most learning game programs which are aimed at a specific grade or age group, this

Chapter 22 : Educational Games

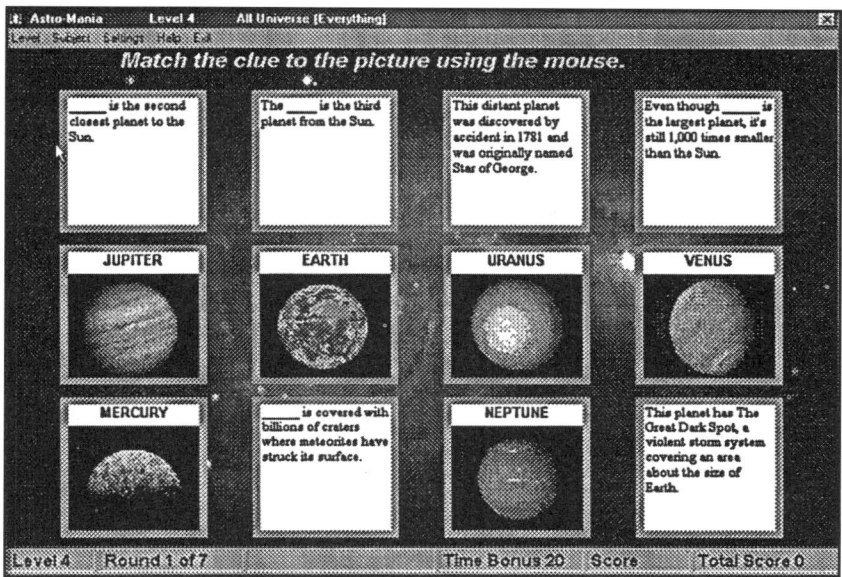

Figure 22.4: A sample screen from level four. Randomly generated questions require matching the text with the image it describes.

program can be useful and fun for anyone, regardless of educational background or grade level. Highly recommended.

Program Name:	Astro Mania® Version 1.5 1998
Program Type:	Shareware (30 day trial period)
Company:	Sheppard Software
Address:	Room 623 Pavilion
	Jenkintown, PA 19046
Web Page:	http://www.sheppardsoftware.com
Registration Fee:	$14.99 on-line or $19.99 by mail.

General Evaluation: DOOM for Windows 95 Launcher

	Excellent	*Good*	*Average*	*Poor*
Level of Challenge	***			
Ability to Maintain Interest	***			
Graphics and Sound	***			
Ease of Learning	***			
Documentation	***			
Overall Rating	***			

Algebra One on One® Version 1.0

If you would like a painless way to review the fundamentals of Algebra, you should definitely give Algebra One on One a try. The program features two different games: Individual Function Practice Game and Algebra Game. The former allows you to practice with each individual function, while the latter requires you to first determine which of several function families is being used, and then solve each equation. Each game can be played in a variety of ways with 21 levels of difficulty.

This program can be of value to anyone who wants to brush up on basic algebra skills, regardless of age. And, while it may not represent a fun game for anyone who dislikes algebra, it can certainly reinforce basic skills in a painless way. It can even allow for competition against a friend, allowing two players to test and exercise their algebra skills, rather than their hand-eye coordination or the quickness of their trigger finger, a refreshing change from the average video game experience.

Program Name: Algebra One on One® Version 1.0 1998
Program Type: Shareware (30 day trial period)
Company: Sheppard Software
E-mail: bradzzzy@aol.com
Address: Room 623 Pavilion
Jenkintown, PA 19046
Web Page: http://www.sheppardsoftware.com
Registration Fee: $14.99 on-line or $29.99 by mail. Faculty can obtain the registered version for school use without cost. For details, contact Sheppard Software at the above e-mail address.

General Evaluation: Algebra One on One Version 1.0

	Excellent	Good	Average	Poor
Level of Challenge	***			
Ability to Maintain Interest	***			
Graphics and Sound			***	
Ease of Learning	***			
Documentation	***			
Overall Rating	***			

I Live At Santa's House® Version 1.5

I Live at Santa's House allows children to fantasize about what it might be like to visit Santa's home and help him make, test, repair and wrap toys, design, bake and eat cookies and even prepare a photo album recording some high points of the visit to leave behind for Santa to remember them by.

While many of the program's features are disabled in the shareware version of this program (decorating the Christmas tree, for example, is limited to selecting a tree topper, packages can only be wrapped in one color scheme, and dolls may be constructed, but not dressed), there are ample activities for children to engage in and four locations for them to explore rendered in attractive graphics accompanied by judicious and effective use of sound effects without background music. There are no learning activities as such, but the whole program helps to teach basic computer skills to young children and to exercise their creativity in such activities as creating and coloring various scenes, repairing broken toys (select and use the glue to repair the loose covering of a box, or choose the hammer to straighten a bent toy carousel), and putting together dolls and stuffed animals by clicking on their separate body parts. In addition, some of the activities reinforce analytical skills and memorization.

In all, this excellent game should appeal to children on a variety of levels beyond the popular Christmas motif, since it provides the opportunity of exploring interesting locales, performing relatively complex tasks, creating, repairing and playing with numerous toys and even exercising some artistic skills in the creation and coloring of cards and in the design of cookies. If testing the activities in this program brought many smiles to this young at heart 41 year old, it will surely bring even broader smiles from the eight and under crowd as they painlessly and enjoyably learn to use a computer to complete some fairly complex tasks.

Program Name: I Live At Santa's House® Version 1.5 1998
Program Type: Shareware (15 day trial period)
Company: AHA! Software Inc.
Address: 1915 Casa Marcia Cr.
Victoria BC V8N 2X4
Canada
E-mail: ssv@familygames.com
Web Page: http://familygames.com
Registration Fee: $20 (Canadian dollars)

Baby Ware® Version 1.0

If you're looking for a delightful program with which to introduce your toddler to the PC, you would be hard pressed to find a nicer one than Baby Ware.

Simple, beautifully rendered graphics and effective use of sound effects and music will have the littlest computer users giggling with delight as they interact with the 12 separate activities. Pressing any key on the keyboard or a mouse button will allow the toddler to interact in some way with each of the activities, such as allowing a mouse to eat a piece of cheese as it walks around the screen, playing hide and seek or peek-a-boo with a little bear.

With the exception of the ESC and F1 keys used to exit programs and provide help, any key pressed by a child has the same effect in each game,

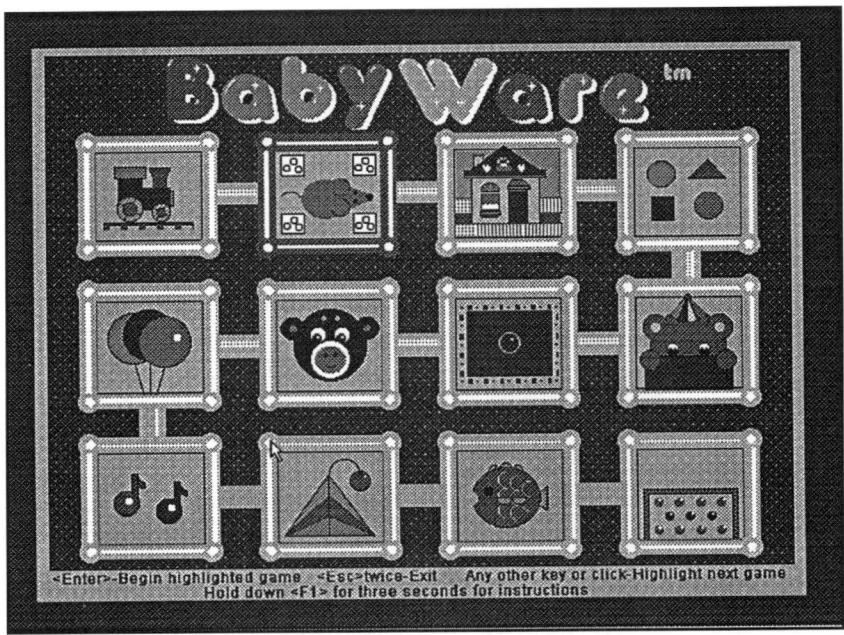

Figure 21.5: *Baby Ware contains 12 distinct activities that allow a child to interact with the game by pressing a key or hitting a mouse button. Fishing, playing hide and seek and helping a bear jump to grab balloons are just three of the activities to choose from. Colorful graphics and baby-paced action should keep a child up to five years old entertained for hours, especially if mom, dad or another loving adult joins in the fun of explaining each activity as they play.*

Chapter 22 : Educational Games

Figure 22.6: Sample activity from Baby Ware. Hitting a key allows the panda bear to jump and capture loose balloons. After capturing three, the panda floats away.

making it easy for a baby to interact with each program. The shareware version of this game is unlimited, but it automatically expires after five uses. If you wish to continue using it after the fifth trial, you must register the game to obtain the key which unlocks the trial version of the program.

Program Name:	Baby Ware® Version 1.0 1998
Program Type:	Shareware Demo (Program expires after 5 trials.)
Copyright Owner:	Patterson-James Interactive, Inc.
Marketed By:	Resilere Corporation
Address:	6404 Wilshire Blvd., Suite 1150
	Los Angeles, CA 90048
E-mail:	babyware@resilere.com
Web Page:	http://www.resilere.com
Registration Fee:	$24.95

General Evaluation: Baby Ware Version 1.0				
	Excellent	*Good*	*Average*	*Poor*
Level of Challenge	***			
Ability to Maintain Interest	***			
Graphics and Sound	***			
Ease of Learning	***			
Documentation			***	
Overall Rating	***			

Fun Flyers: Jet® Version 1.0 (Single Plane Version)

Anyone interested in learning about the science of flight in general, and military jet aircraft in particular, should try this unique program that offers a brief primer on the principles of flight along with detailed information on ten popular military aircraft. Best of all, this program allows anyone with access to a computer, printer, some glue and a little patience to make their own flying model airplane.

This demo version of the program allows any user to personalize and print detailed plans and instructions for building a flying model of an F-16 Falcon. Any user can, by following the clear, concise instructions, cut out the necessary parts from a template printed by the program, glue and assemble the necessary parts together to create a working model that the program's creators claim can, under the proper wind conditions, fly for more than 100 yards when launched by a catapult rubber band launcher easily built by following the program's instructions.

This evaluation version of the program includes minimal graphics and no sound files, but it does contain specifications for all ten planes. In addition to plans for all ten planes, the full version of the program includes video of all planes and enhanced graphics and sound, as well as heavy duty paper to make flying versions of all ten military aircraft and a rubber band launcher. In addition, the full version of the program permits printing of airport layouts and planes onto paper or onto iron-on transfer sheets.

The program is suitable for anyone at least eight years of age, and requires a 486-class CPU or better running Windows 95/98 with at least 32 MB of RAM and 20 MB of free disk space.

Chapter 22 : Educational Games

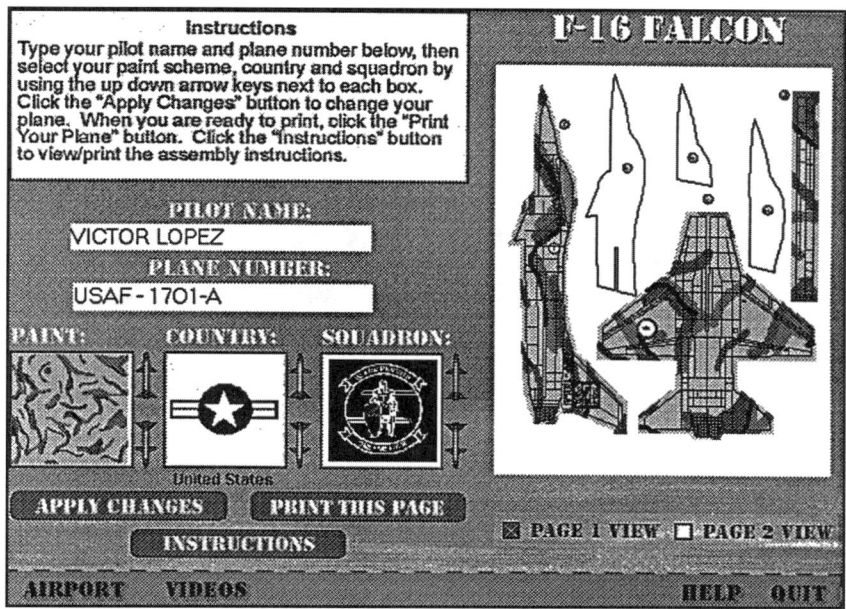

Figure 22.7: *With a color printer and some care, the finished product can not only fly well but look good, too. Regardless of whether a color or monochrome printer is used, care must be taken in cutting, gluing and assembling all parts if the finished product is to function well. Unlike most familiar paper airplanes, this program achieves the necessary aerodynamics and structural strength not by folding paper, but rather by constructing a body out of layers of paper (eight layers for parts of the fuselage) carefully glued together.*

Program Name:	Fun Flyers: Jets® Version 1.0 (Single Plane Version) 1998
Program Type:	Demo
Company:	KittyHawk Software, Inc.
Address:	PO Box 64189
	Tucson, AZ 85728
E-mail:	support@khs.com
Web Page:	http://www.khs.com/khs/
Registration Fee:	$29.95 plus shipping

General Evaluation: Fun Flyers: Jet Version 1.0

	Excellent	Good	Average	Poor
Level of Challenge	***			
Ability to Maintain Interest	***			

	Excellent	Good	Average	Poor
Graphics and Sound		***		
Ease of Learning	***			
Documentation	***			
Overall Rating	***			

Ray's Numbers Game® Version 3.1

Ray's Numbers Game allows children to practice their basic math skills (addition, subtraction, multiplication and division) in a fun, competitive environment.

Playing the game is simple: after selecting the type of activity and setting the difficulty level, a game grid appears on the screen that consists of a series of numbers laid out in a square pattern for both the player and the computer opponent. Each then takes turns solving a math problem at one of three speed settings. Once the problem is solved, the answer is selected by clicking on it with the mouse. If the answer is correct, one of three symbols appears (horseshoe, heart or smiling face); if it is incorrect, the player gets another chance to choose the correct answer, time permitting. If time expires or more than one incorrect answer is selected, the correct answer appears, along with a sad face graphic. Correct answers are rewarded with a happy face graphic, and the correct answer is replaced by one of the three symbols previously noted. The first to accumulate four symbols of a kind wins the game.

The shareware version of this program provides two skill levels: lower and intermediate. The lower level permits basic counting (up to 14), and addition and subtraction involving the numbers 0–7. The intermediate level allows for practice with addition and subtraction involving numbers from 0–100, and multiplication and division involving numbers up to 6. The registered version of the program provides an advanced level that covers working with fractions, decimals and percentages and expands the customizable features of lower levels (e.g., it allows multiplication and division involving numbers up to 12) and activates tutorials that are disabled in the shareware version. Additional features of the program include the ability to practice multiplication tables before (but not during) game play.

Overall, this is a neat software package that will allow children to hone their basic arithmetic skills in friendly competition against a computer that, in a very un-computer like fashion, will sometimes make mistakes or fail to answer a question on time (giving even children with less than per-

Chapter 22 : Educational Games

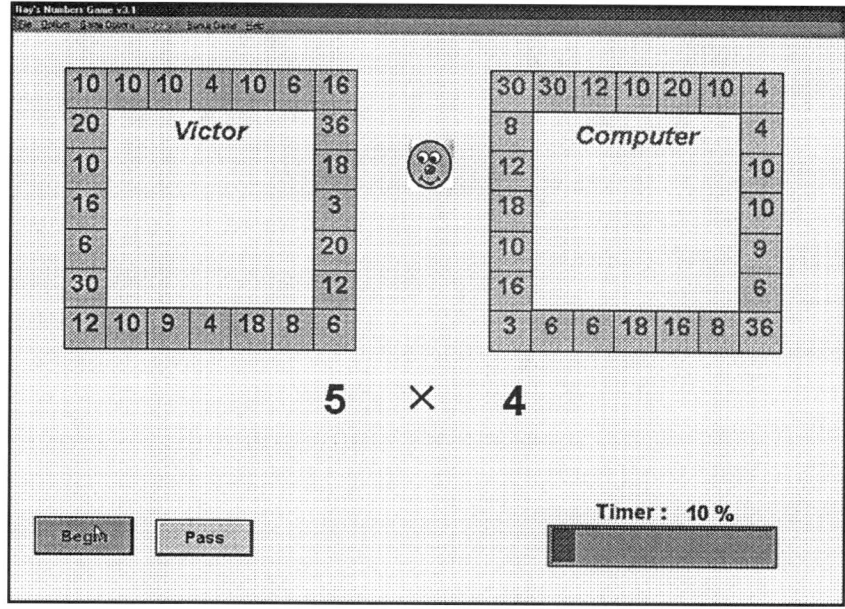

Figure 22.8: Practicing basic arithmetic skills is a snap with Ray's Numbers Game. Multiplication and division of two numbers from 0–6 are supported. Bonus games are also available as a reward for winning, including a memory matching game that requires matching hidden pairs of items within a present period of time.

fect skills the ability to beat the computer once in a while). Graphics and sounds are sedate, but help to enhance what is essentially a repetitive math drill, allowing children to enjoy the experience of working out basic arithmetic problems "in their heads" (or on paper in the slower setting).

Program Name:	Ray's Numbers Game® Version 3.1 1996-1999
Program Type:	Shareware (30 day license)
Copyright Owner:	Ray Le Couteur
Address:	Ray Le Couteur Educational
	47 Daffodil Way
	Chilmsford, Essex CM1 6XB
	U.K.
E-mail:	RayLec@compuserve.com
Phone :	1-800-242-4775 Extension 15280 (within the U.S.)
	1-713-524-6394 Extension 15280 (outside of the U.S.)
Registration Fee:	£12 ($20 U.S.)

General Evaluation: Ray's Numbers Game Version 3.1				
	Excellent	*Good*	*Average*	*Poor*
Level of Challenge		***		
Ability to Maintain Interest	***			
Graphics and Sound			***	
Ease of Learning	***			
Documentation	***			
Overall Rating	***			

Ray's Spelling and Word Games® Version 2.0

Children who need to work on their spelling will find Ray's Spelling and Word Games a fun and productive activity. The program permits three different learning activities: Spelling, Find the Word and Word Jumble.

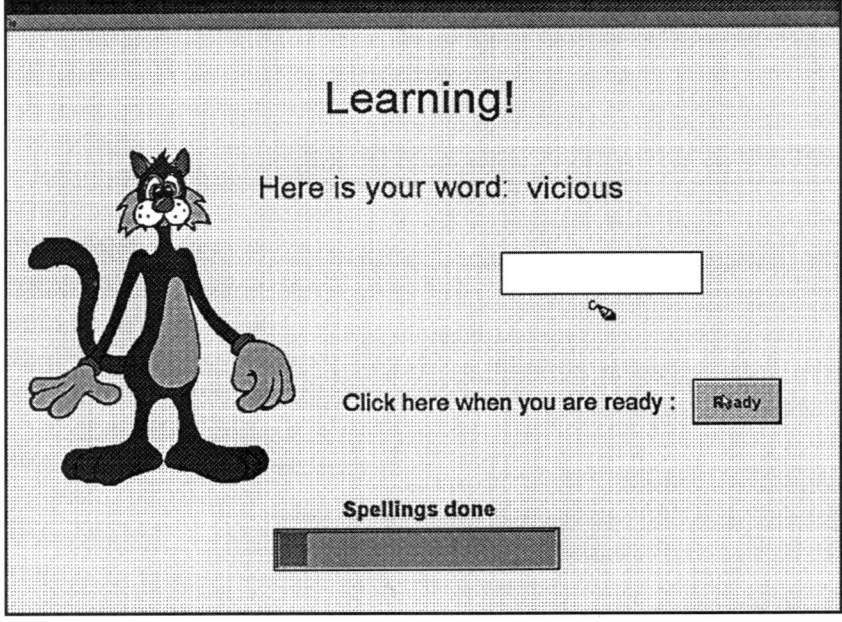

Figure 22.9: *The Spelling module provides the opportunity to learn, practice and be tested in new words. A word is flashed (and spoken, if it was recorded when entered), then the user has the chance to spell it. Words that are misspelled are flagged for further practice. Adding words is a simple process that makes this a highly customizable module, rather than a generic spelling practice program.*

Chapter 22 : Educational Games

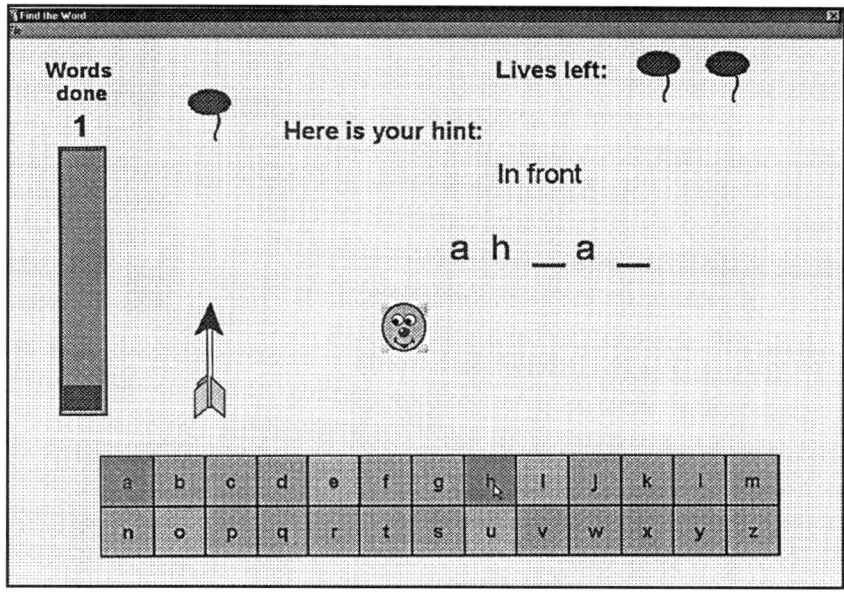

Figure 22.10: The Find the Word module requires a user to spell a word before the balloon falls onto the spear at the left of the screen. A hint helps to identify the word, and letters for its spelling are selected from the alphabet grid at the bottom of the screen. If a letter appears more than once in the word (such as the letter "a" in "ahead" in this example) it will automatically be placed everywhere it appears in the word at once.

In the Spelling activity, a user can enter any words to be studied, and optionally record the pronunciation of the words, with the student then having the opportunity to practice spelling these words after the program flashes each word and pronounces it. The difficulty of each drill can be customized to any student's level, with the process of entering new words both simple and intuitive.

The Find the Word activity requires the user to spell out a word after reading a clue about it. The user selects letters from a grid by clicking on them; if the letter recurs more than once in the word, it is placed in its proper place on the dotted line below the word's description (see Figure 22.18). Quick thinking is necessary, especially with more difficult words, since the activity is timed. A balloon descends slowly at the left of the screen onto a sharp spear as time passes and drops sharply a short distance every wrong guess. Three balloons are available, a the game ends when all three have burst. The more words that can be correctly defined before all three balloons are spent, the higher the score a user will achieve.

Unit V : Games

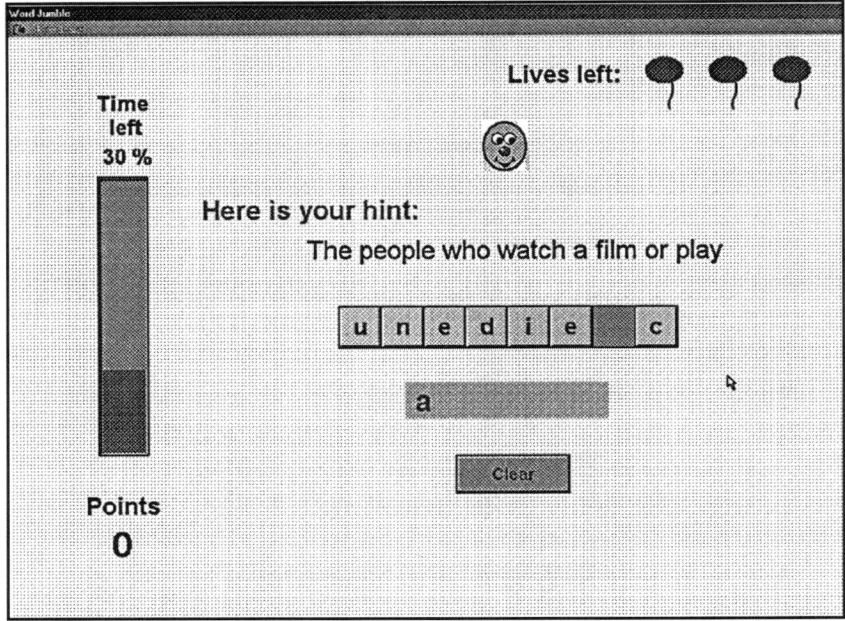

Figure 22.11: In the Word Jumble module, a player must decipher the jumbled word within approximately one minute. After 30% of the time has expired, a hint about the word is given, as seen here. Failure to guess the first letter after approximately half the time has expired will yield one final hint: the first letter of the word. Even after recognizing a word, such as the word "audience" in this example, it must be keyed in by clicking on each letter in the sequence it should appear.

As with most games, high scores are recorded for posterity, serving as marks to be surpassed as a player's spelling and word recognition skills improve.

The final module, Word Jumble, provides perhaps the greatest challenge, forcing a player to concentrate and see word patterns that are not always obvious. When 30% of the time allowed has elapsed, a hint relating to the word pops onto the screen, helping the user to deduce the meaning of the jumbled letters. If the user is still unable to decipher the word, the first letter of the word pops up a short time thereafter. With longer words, even experienced users will be challenged to see the pattern and type in the necessary letters on time while racing to beat the clock.

Although the shareware version of this game contains limitations, such as Word Jumble and Find the Word lists that are limited to 50 words, the available features allow for an ample (and very useful) trial during the evaluation period. Overall, this program provides a good balance of instruction and entertainment that can help sharpen both spelling skills and concentration skills for students of various grade levels.

Program Name:	Ray's Spelling and Word Games® Version 2.0 1996-1998
Program Type:	Shareware (30 day license)
Copyright Owner:	Ray Le Couteur
Address:	Ray Le Couteur Educational
	47 Daffodil Way
	Chilmsford, Essex CM1 6XB
	U.K. **E-mail:** RayLec@compuserve.com
Phone:	1-800-242-4775 Extension 15280 (within the U.S.)
	1-713-524-6394 Extension 15280 (outside of the U.S.)
Registration Fee:	12 ($20 U.S.)

General Evaluation: Ray's Spelling and Word Games Version 2.0

	Excellent	Good	Average	Poor
Level of Challenge	***			
Ability to Maintain Interest	***			
Graphics and Sound	***			
Ease of Learning		***		
Documentation		***		
Overall Rating	***			

INDEX

ABC Treehouse 186
AceReader 98, 101
Action Games 131, 134, 136, 137, 139
address book 83
AHA! Software Inc. 191
Algebra One on One 190
Alien Ambush 147
The All-In-One Mortgage Calculator 67, 69
Ambertec, Inc. 153
America Online, Inc. 118
American Systems 40
amortization schedule 63, 65
amortization table 65, 66
AndroSoft. 20
Ant Run Pro 149
AOLPress 117, 118
Apogee 136, 137
Arachnophilia 119, 121
arcade-style games 147
arithmetic skills 196
Arouza, Kevin 49
Astro Mania 188
astronomy 188
attendance 106, 108–111
authors' web pages 5

Baby Ware 192
backup program 48, 76
Battleship 173
BCWipe 43, 45
bitmap images 71
Bloch, John 165

Bloch Reversi 165
BMP file 18, 21
Bollinger, Alfred 71
browser enhancement tools 116

Calypso 52, 53
Canasta for Windows 95/98/NT 175
Card Games 175, 177, 181, 182
CareWare 120, 121
CD-ROM collections 5
ChalkSoft 105
ChalkSoft's Courseware Web 102, 105
checkers 160, 162, 163
chess 160–162
Chgname 50, 52
compressed archives 14, 16
computer-based multiple choice exams 94
computer-based testing 91
computer literacy 93, 107, 115
Computer Training & Support Corporation 93
configuration file backup 41
Connect It 169
contacts database 87
Cool Mouse 59
copyright protection 3
courseware 89, 102, 105

database program 86, 88
Deberdt, Rene-Gilles 167
debt to income ratio 67
demo programs 3, 4, 6, 7, 155
DirectX 154, 155

Index

Disk Utilities 36
DiveSpaceCheck 36
Doom for Windows 95 Launcher 131
Doom 131
DOOM II 132
DOS 1, 14, 19, 20, 23, 41, 43, 70, 72, 102, 129, 131, 132
Duplication Factory 37, 38

E.G. Chess 160
Earth Gaming 161
educational games 186
educational programs 89, 186
electronic grade book 110
EliaShim, Inc. 29
Elite Air Hockey 158
ESP Data Solutions, Inc. 64
exam production 93
Executive Desk '97 83, 86

F-16 Falcon 194
FastWare 16
FASTZip 98 16
file compression 9, 11, 12, 16, 26, 48, 52
file creation date 51
file management 52
file synchronization 45
File Utilities 43, 52
first-person perspective 135, 139, 142
Fodera, Tony 46
Forty Thieves 177
Free and User Supported Software for the IBM PC: A Resource Guide for Libraries and Individuals 1, 2
free software collections 7
Free Solitaire 177
freeware 2–7, 11, 14–16, 18, 21, 32, 34, 36, 37, 42, 43, 45, 46, 49, 52, 56, 60, 64, 70, 71, 74, 79, 80, 89, 105, 115, 116, 118, 120, 125–128, 168, 177, 181
FTP 11, 22, 125
Fun Flyers: Jet 194

Games 83, 129–132, 134, 136, 137, 139, 141, 143–145, 147–149, 154, 158, 160, 163, 167, 168, 170, 175, 177, 180–183, 186, 190, 198, 200, 201
Games of Strategy 160, 168
Gerety, Adam 69
GradeStar Version 110
Grading Programs 89, 106, 107
graphics acceleration 129, 140
Gupta, Sumit 123

hard disk problems 36
Henrik Holdt 82
Hexen 131
Hexen II 134
hotspot answer selection 92
HTML 71, 102, 103, 117, 119, 122, 128, 136, 161, 167
HTML programming 103, 117, 119, 122, 128
Hypertext Markup Language 117

I Live At Santa's House 191
id Software, Inc. 136, 142
Indigo Rose Corporation 38
infected files 23
Instant Messenger 128
Internet 6, 7, 12, 22, 23, 25, 26, 29, 36, 50, 79, 102, 115, 124–128, 155, 158
Internet Explorer 5.0 125, 126
Internet Tools 115
Interplay Productions, Ltd. 157
Interrupt Infinity 56
iSBiSTER International, Inc. 88

J. Ollman & Associates 181
JB Systems 42
JSpades 181

Kai, Kevin 66
Kintrup, Frank 77
Kirillov, Kirill M. 60
KittyHawk Software, Inc. 195
Kyodai 166

Lanford, Scott 78
Le Couter, Ray 197, 201
librarians 7
licensing information 3
LifeSaver 41, 42
Livshits, Vitaly 172
loan amortization 64, 65
Loan Calculators 63
Lotus 1, 2, 64
LucasArts Entertainment Company 142, 145, 149, 153, 155
Lutus, Paul 120, 121

MaeDae Enterprises 95
Mag Lense 95
Mah Jongg 166
Master Mind 170
McAfee Associates, Inc. 23, 26, 29
Michael McCulloch 181

Index

Microsoft 1, 2, 6, 58, 87, 103, 116, 122–126, 154, 155, 175
Microsoft Excel 58
Microsoft Exchange 87
Microsoft Explorer 58, 116, 124
Microsoft Power Point 103
Microsoft Word 58, 103
Milori Software 97
Mind's Tic Tac Toe 167
mouse utilities 9, 55
MousePad 55, 56
multimedia presentations 95
multiple choice tests 93
multiple disk copies 37

Nestegg Software 21
Netscape 6, 116, 124, 125, 127, 128
Netscape Communicator 116, 124, 127, 128
NetWatch 127
Niko Mak Computing, Inc. 13
Noisy Video Poker/Blackjack for Windows 95 182
Norton AntiVirus 26, 28
Norton Utilities 43
Nostrum India 123
Nygård, Kjetil L. 52

Outlaws 142

Parks, Donovan 168
Patterson-James Interactive, Inc. 193
PC Chalkboard 95–97
Pentium III 129, 130
periodic payments on a loan 64
Perpetual Motion Enterprises, Inc. 158
Personal Information Management 83, 86
personal productivity 61, 98
Pharaoh's Ascent 151
phone book dialer 88
Pipe Dreams 149
PKUNZIP 11
Platform for Internet Content Selection (PICS) 127
Plus700 162
Pointix 57, 58
Pointix Corporation 58
Print Screen key 18, 70, 72
printer configuration 73
printer management tasks 70
Printer Tools 70
PrintKey 70, 71
Printscreen 95 72, 73
program launcher 85

public domain software 2
Pyramid 151, 177

Quake II 139, 143
Quake III 132, 139, 140
Quick Quote 63, 64
Quick Sound 95, 97

racing simulation 156
Rapid Serial Visual Presentation (RSVP) 98
Ray Le Couteur Educational 197, 201
Ray's Numbers Game 196
Ray's Spelling and Word Games 198
read-only files 45
recycle bin 39, 43
Reid, Bill 37
Resilere Corporation 193
Reversi 164, 165
Rich Text Format 119
RoundClock 76, 77

Screen Capture 21
screen capture 9, 18–21
screen capture/print 72
screen capture utilities 18, 19
Sea Haven Towers 177
SeaSide Studios 170
seating charts 109, 112
The SGN/Starline Company 148
shareware 2–7, 9, 12, 13, 18, 20, 24, 26, 29, 34, 36, 40–42, 53, 58, 66, 69, 73, 74, 77, 78, 80, 82, 86–89, 95, 97, 101, 105, 109, 111, 112, 115–117, 120, 123, 125, 127, 131, 132, 136–139, 150, 155, 161, 163, 165, 167, 170–172, 174–176, 183, 184, 189–191, 193, 196, 197, 200, 201
shareware distributors 3
shareware download sites 5
ShellTech Software Corp. 112
Sheppard Software 189, 190
Sight & Sound 53
Soleau Software, Inc. 150
solitaire games 83, 175, 177
Sources of Freeware, Shareware and Demo Programs 5
space combat 153, 154
Space Invaders 147
Speed Reading 89, 98
Spider 177
Spiral Enterprises 1, LLC 188
Splitit95 47, 49
SPX/IPX 132
Star Wars 153

Startsev, Serge 164
StepWare, Inc. 101
Submarine 2 173
SuperClip 18, 20
Super Simple Software 73
Symantec 26, 28, 29
Symantec Corporation 28
Syncer! 45, 46
system analysis 9, 32
system's clock 79, 80

Tachistoscopic Scroll Presentation 98, 99
Tarantula 122, 123
TCP/IP 132
telephone book 86, 87
Ternovski, Dimitri 15
test construction 91–93
Test Construction Set 91, 93
test delivery 91
Testing and Training Aids 91
third mouse 59
3D action games 131, 134, 137, 139
3D graphics accelerator 129, 139
3D Realms Entertainment 137, 139, 176
Tic Tac Toe 160, 167, 168
TidyDisk 39, 40
Time & Chaos 32 86, 88
Time95 80, 82
TimeRC 79, 80
Time Tools 76
Timex Data Link 86
Training Tools 95, 97
True Test 93, 95

Ultimate Software, Inc. 184
Ultra Logic 170
U.S. Department of Defense 115
USysWare 74
utility programs 9, 12, 16, 32, 43
utility suite 91, 95

Vajn, Krešimir 174
VAR Grade for Windows 95 107, 109
VARed Software 109
Video Blackjack 182–184
Video Poker 182–184
viral infections 13, 29
virtual keyboard 55
virus definition 23, 27, 29
virus detection 9, 22, 23, 25, 26, 29
Virus Scan 22, 23, 25, 26
ViruSafe 95 29
Voice Clock 78
VR Sports Powerboat Racing Demo 156

web browsers 12, 120, 124, 125, 127
Web Page Creation 117
what if calculations 64
Windows 2000 125
Windows 95/98 1, 5, 9, 12, 14, 18, 23, 32, 36, 39, 43, 51, 61, 70, 73, 76, 79, 91, 102, 110, 112, 131, 132, 145, 150, 154, 156, 160, 175–177, 188, 194
Windows Clipboard 18, 71, 99
Windows Explorer 11, 13, 14, 21, 40, 43, 52, 63, 103
Windows Magazine 32, 34
Windows Paint 18
Wintune 97 34
Wintune 98 32, 34
WinZip 12, 13
Wolfenstein 3D 131
Word Jumble 198, 200
world clock program 80
world time clock 85
World Wide Web 23, 98, 115
WPrinter Lite 73, 74

X-Wing Alliance Demo 153